To

I KNOW YOU WILL

ENJOY THIS BOOK.

IT WAS TOO MUCH

FUN!!!

ENJOY!

[illegible signature]

2008

From the Rearview Mirror

First Professional, Then Private.

Ride along in the limousine as you read these short stories told through the eyes of a chauffeur.

Ric Castorano

authorHOUSE®

AuthorHouse™
1663 Liberty Drive, Suite 200
Bloomington, IN 47403
www.authorhouse.com
Phone: 1-800-839-8640

First published by AuthorHouse 10/16/2007

ISBN: 978-1-4343-4046-7 (sc)

Library of Congress Control Number: 2007907721

Printed in the United States of America
Bloomington, Indiana

This book is printed on acid-free paper.

This work is dedicated to my life partner
who lived every driving experience
as it happened.
Thank you for your ongoing love and support.

This work is also dedicated to my mother, Anna. She was a kind-hearted, generous woman and the matriarch of our family. She was constantly organizing family gatherings until her death on her forty-seventh wedding anniversary, April 27, 1993. In her own way, she supported all of my decisions and ambitions. As I would tell her about my experiences, she always would say, *"you should put that in a book."*
Well Mom, here it is!

Finally, I would like to thank my many friends for their continued support and encouragement for my completion of this work. Although too numerous to mention, you know who you are.

THANK YOU ALL!

Enjoy!

TABLE OF CONTENTS

INTRODUCTION

The stories you are about to venture into are a series of experiences that I had while driving as a chauffeur. I initially worked as a professional chauffeur for a limousine company for about six years, and later as a private chauffeur for a period of about ten months. During those time periods, I met a wide variety of characters, some of which you will meet as you read each chapter. The first ten chapters are taken from situations I found myself in while working for the limousine company. These chapters were a lot of fun to write and were written to make you feel as though you were riding along in the car. The last chapter, "The Golden Opportunity," is my experience in driving as a private chauffeur for a local doctor and his wife, which was the last job of my driving career. This work will unmask the many faces of the public; some are good and some are bad, which is why I have chosen to change the names of the characters throughout. If you have ever thought of becoming a limousine driver, these short stories may help you decide. Whether you have rented a limousine or have wanted to, you'll easily be able to imagine yourself in the driver's seat, and you'll always remember that the driver is watching your every move from the rearview mirror.

As you read along for the ride, don't forget your seat belt—it's the law!

THE SILVER CLOUD II

So started another week of work. Like millions of people, I really hated Monday mornings. Being in my late twenties, I was still trying to figure out just exactly what I wanted to do with my life; I believe everyone goes through that type of self-evaluation. Some never find it; most settle for a compromise. I kept hoping that a job would come along that I would enjoy and be good at. Of course, I wanted to make a lot of money as well. That is a tough combination to come up with if you don't know for sure what you want to do with your life.

I was taught that when you get a job, you should hold on to it; you should never leave it or change, because that doesn't look good. That's great if you're happy with the same old daily grind like my father was. He retired from the one and only job he had after forty-seven years as a drill press operator at a local quarry. He would go to work every day, put his eight hours in, and be home by 4:30 p.m., where mom always had supper ready by 5:00 p.m. Then he would read the newspaper and fall asleep by 9:00 p.m. in his easy chair. From there, he would go to bed by 11:00 p.m. so he could start his day over. He would do that day in and day out! This drove me absolutely crazy, because he was never able to do things with us unless it was Saturday or Sunday, and even then his time was divided between the church and chores in the garden. My parents dedicated their lives to serving the Church. They worked at the church Bingo on Tuesday and Saturday nights and went to Mass every Sunday. Mom was also the head of the women's club, which was not an easy position to hold. But they found happiness in that world. I grew up in a large Italian family; there were always relatives or neighbors stopping by. At times our house seemed like Grand Central Station; there was always someone coming or going. It also seemed as though they could smell mom's spaghetti sauce and meatballs cooking, as their timing was perfect. There were times when it was fun, but basically we had little privacy in our lives. Though there were nine kids in mom's family and eleven in dad's, our immediate family was small, as I had only one sibling. My brother was just over three years older than I, and as kids he took every chance to tease me in the usual fashion that older siblings do. Of course, he has never seen it from my perspective and never will. I'm told he felt and was treated like an only child because he was the first-born child. It seemed to me that my parents would never stop him unless *they* were irritated to the point of having had enough. My mother would yell at him, but almost every time I was in trouble, my brother was behind it.

I learned early in life that I held the key to my survival and that there had to be more than this daily grind that my parents were so happy with, so I began to look for my own path in life. I wanted to be different; you know, I wanted to stand out and do something special to be remembered for. I saw a lot of people living up to others' perceptions and standards or doing things because they would look good. I basically didn't care what anyone thought; I knew I had to search for and carve a path to call my own. I hadn't gone to college; I had listened to my parents complain that college would cost a lot of money. That turned out to be the biggest mistake of my life, since most employers want to see a degree, and now you have to have a master's of some sort to even stand out in the crowd. I briefly worked in a factory, following in the footsteps of my brother, who helped me secure that position. It was an experience to say the least, and it just wasn't a good fit for me.

After answering an ad in the newspaper, I was hired at a law firm as an office clerk. I had only been working there for about a month when I realized that it was no place to have a rewarding career. I was looking for a job, as everyone does, that was interesting and, of course, profitable.

When I came to the law firm for the interview, I was very impressed as I looked around the office. I had never been in any office that had such structure. I was intrigued by the associates as I watched people hustling around and as I listened to the employees talking on the phones. It was a collection law firm, so I could hear the collectors threatening people on the phone to make payments on their overdue balances. The collectors were threatening to repossess cars, motorcycles, and boats and to foreclose on their houses. They talked of filing bank attachments on any account they could find and garnishing their wages. At times I really felt sorry for the people on the other ends of the phones. After working there for the short period, I realized that there were those deadbeats that obviously had their priorities misplaced and shrugged off their financial commitments by not making any payments toward their outstanding debts. One woman told a collector that God would take care of her bills. A couple that I knew from the neighborhood where I grew up came into the office. Their daughter had recently been married, and the unpaid bill for the wedding totaled over fourteen thousand dollars. They charged everything on credit cards, and the wife was hiding the bills from her husband. I have to admit, it was a beautiful wedding. Of course I didn't want them to see me in that office, so I hid behind a file cabinet and asked someone else to wait on them. The people that really got to me were the ones that had lost their jobs and had trouble regaining employment because their professions had been outsourced to other countries. It was very tough listening to the hardship stories, but it was a job, and as harsh as it sounds, I became numb to it after a short time. My particular function was to notarize the legal documents that would be filed in the courts around the state to attach bank accounts, garnish wages, and repossess property. I would notarize as the attorneys would sign, and then the documents were either filed at the local courthouse or mailed to courthouses around the state.

The young woman that initially interviewed me came across as very nice; her name was Betty, and she would end up being my supervisor. She was in her mid-twenties, and she seemed to be quite educated. She was also attempting to pass the entrance exam for law school, and she gave the impression that she would do well. When she talked to me, I quickly learned of her qualities. She had certain characteristics of a viper that are required of an attorney; I thought she might make it. The more I listened to her and saw her in action in the office, the more I began to realize that this was not a person to be on the bad side of. She was in the process of a divorce, and the failure of the marriage was really getting to her, and she felt embarrassed about it. I later learned from her that her husband had left her for another man. Well, that set the stage for her to become a very bitter woman. According to her, she blamed her husband for everything, and as she put it, "no man would ever be good enough" for her. I discovered quickly that I did not want to be associated with her, but I needed to stay on her good side. The building that our office was located in was in an old, worn-down area on the south edge of downtown. Several years after my employment there ended, the entire area was renovated. It is referred to now as the Brewery District in midtown. It is now one of the more expensive neighborhoods in the city. The office didn't look like much; it was cold and very pale in appearance. This branch had just opened, and they were trying to make it look nice. A little paint and new carpet would do wonders, but that, of course, would take away from the profits.

I often wandered off at lunch by myself just for some peace and quiet and a little alone time. One day, while working in the office, I heard some of my coworkers on the opposite side of the room talking about a car in the parking lot just below our windows. We were on the second floor of the building, and when you looked out, you could see the lot. So like everyone else, I went over to see what it was. As I approached the window, I saw the biggest and most beautiful shiny silver Rolls Royce four door. It turned out to be a 1962 Rolls Royce Silver Cloud II. The car was painted metallic silver and had a blood red leather interior and thick, gangster-style whitewall tires. We also noticed that the car was right-hand drive; a true English gem. Words could not describe how beautiful this automobile was, but being a car buff, I knew I had to get closer. It seemed as if I couldn't control myself; something was drawing me to that car, and I knew I had to go to the parking lot to get a closer look. The closer I got to the car, the more I thought to myself that I would someday drive that incredible car. It was long, and it had obviously just been washed, as there was not a speck of dirt to be seen on it. I must have looked like an idiot while just standing there and peering into the car windows. The wood on the dashboard and the door panels was beautifully hand crafted; the wood veneer on the dashboard was split, which created a mirror image on the right and the left sides. The post holding the rearview mirror extended from the dashboard, unlike they do in most cars, where they extend down from the ceiling. The seats were of thick plush and leather and had beautiful wood grain pullout tray tables for anyone sitting in the back seat. That vintage car was in perfect condition, and as I stood there, I expected someone to come out yelling at me to get away from it, but that didn't happen. I looked over the car for about twenty minutes, noticing the fine craftsmanship in every detail. I thought to myself, *I have got to meet the person who owns this car.* I looked around, not knowing whom or where the owner was, and I began walking around the area. There were several bars and shops close by, which were where I began my hunt. I soon came upon a hair salon next to one of the bars, and when I walked by the window, I could see a woman in a tuxedo getting her hair cut. I thought to myself that she must have been driving that car; she looked like a chauffeur. Since I knew one of the stylists that worked in the salon, I walked in to chat with him and to maybe strike up a conversation about the Rolls Royce. Tim was the barber that I knew, and after chatting with him for a few minutes, he introduced me to the woman in the tuxedo. I asked if that was her car out back. She said the car actually belonged to her fiancé and that he needed a driver that afternoon for a booking. He was starting a limo business, and he owned one Rolls Royce. It was the only Rolls Royce–only limousine service at that time. She went on to mention that he worked full-time on the third shift at a brewery and also remodeled homes for resale in the area. So, being as bold as I could be, and having gone this far to find out what I could about the car, I jokingly said to her, "is he looking for any more drivers?" She laughed, looked at me, and said, "Yes, as a matter of fact he is." I told her that I was very interested in a part-time driving job and that I would love to talk to him. She gave me his phone number and asked me to call him that evening. We chatted for the duration of her haircut, and then I had to get back to work. She said that she would mention our conversation to her fiancé that evening so he would be expecting my call.

I went back to the office floating with pride, and I had the biggest smile on my face as I walked in the door. Little did I know the whole office had been watching out of the windows as I walked to the Rolls with the chauffeur. No one in the office could believe that I boldly went in to talk to the driver, not to mention that I had tried to secure a part-time chauffeuring job as well. Actually, from the sounds of some of their comments, I thought that a few of them were jealous. I especially enjoyed the look on Betty's face as it registered what I had done. It told me that she was about to do or say something stupid.

I had never even been in a limousine, but this was a classic Rolls Royce, and better yet, there was a possibility of me driving it. I was so excited that I told everyone back at the office that I had the owner's phone number and that his fiancée had told me to call him about a job, which I planned to do that evening. I truly was acting like a child at Christmas. The only thing that Betty could say was, "be sure to call from home and not during work." I could have wrapped that phone cord around her neck. I would often daydream thinking of ways to inflict slow pain upon her.

That night, when I called the owner of the limousine company, he mentioned the conversation

I'd had with his fiancée. He was interested in meeting me and having another driver. As we talked, he asked several questions about my driving habits as well as my driving record. You can understand how concerned he would be about having someone drive his twenty-five-year-old Rolls Royce. I told him that my driving record was perfect and that I had never received as much as a parking ticket. He asked for my personal information to verify any violations with the bureau of motor vehicles and then he said he would call me back. I, too, would check out anyone driving my car, especially since they would be driving passengers around and serving champagne.

The next day, while I was working like a dog at the law firm, I received a call from Ed, the owner of the limousine service. He said that my driving and criminal records checked out as well as my references, and he asked me to come over; he wanted to meet with me to take a test drive in the Rolls. I couldn't wait!

Ed operated his business out of his garage and house, and the area that he lived in was close to where I worked at the law firm. It was in the same area of the largest private restoration project in the United States. Once the homes there were renovated, they were beautiful and very expensive.

People were making great profits on the refurbished homes, and I would find out later that Ed did a lot of work on his property himself. It was clearly reflected in his work. He didn't care much for anything except the money he could make off of a venture or anyone that he could get to do work for him at a cheap rate. He specialized in renovating repossessed houses in depressed areas that one could buy for a dollar or else very cheaply. It was a great way to start the rebuilding of neighborhoods, though. Later that evening, I arrived at Ed's house. (I was on time, by the way. I was *always* on time, which is a prerequisite of the job.) We hit it off immediately and headed to the garage where the Rolls Royce was kept. He opened the door and there it was, that beautiful 1962 Silver Cloud II Rolls Royce. It was an awesome sight, taking up every inch of the garage. I couldn't believe anyone drove it into the garage, as it appeared to be such a tight fit. When I mentioned how beautiful it was, Ed mentioned that it was good I noticed that, because washing it and keeping it clean was also part of the job. That would not be a problem, because I loved vintage cars and had grown up working on my own. Ed tossed the keys to the Rolls to me and asked me if I thought I could back it out of the garage. Since it was right-hand drive and very expensive, I thought I would let him pull it out of the garage until I was able to drive it and get a feel for how it handled. Once it was out of the garage, I got behind the wheel, remembering to enter the car on the right side, which was very odd at first. It felt awkward driving with the steering wheel on the right side; not only are you on the opposite side of the car, but the dashboard is also backwards. My nerves were on edge to say the least, but I pulled into traffic. It felt as though I was piloting a cruise ship, and it moved very gracefully. The car handled so well that I quickly overcame any anxiety and fear of it and started to relax and enjoy driving it. Ed was impressed with my driving; he noticed my smooth acceleration and my braking to soft stops. These are qualities you must have to drive as a chauffeur. With clients riding in the back seat, you can't stomp on the gas to take off, nor can you jam on the brakes to stop. If you did either, you would have whiplash victims and would be tossing your passengers all over the back seat.

Everyone has ridden with someone that has no sympathy for his or her passengers. When this happens, you feel like a milkshake when you get out of the car, or you feel the need for something to stop the motion sickness.

Ed mentioned that I was doing a great job, and he said that I passed his test, which made him feel very confident and comfortable with me behind the wheel. The next thing he wanted to talk about was the presentation of the car at churches for weddings and the presentation of the champagne at curbside.

There was a hand-painted reversible sign that was kept in the trunk of the car and could be attached to the rear bumper. It said "Just Married" on one side and "Happy Birthday" on the other side. It wasn't very professional looking at all, but Ed had made it, and he thought it was nice. I would have thought that a professional print job would have been in order, but that wasn't the case.

Ed's performance of standing by the car and opening the champagne bottle seemed like a magic act or a mime performance. It was ridiculously funny, and I tried not to laugh out loud. But he showed me how he wanted it to be done, and I repeated it for him while he acted like a proud father. It really was silly looking, and when I did do it as he suggested, people chuckled. My presentation was just as impressive, and it seemed more professional and natural. I thought of myself as being the kind of chauffeur that anyone would want to drive him or her around, not as a stuffed shirt. I wanted to be a cool chauffeur, and I wanted to enjoy the job at the same time.

The next step was to buy a tuxedo (at my own cost, by the way) and then I would be ready for my first driving assignment.

While keeping the job at the law firm, I was a part-time chauffeur in the evenings and on weekends. Little did I know this part-time chauffeuring job was going to expose me to all types of people and put me into some pretty precarious situations.

As I write about some of the things that happened, good and bad, I realize that I wouldn't trade the experience for anything. Shortly after being hired, I met the other driver, who also worked part-time. His name was Dean, and he was a very colorful character to say the least.

CELEBRITY COUNT

Throughout my driving career I had the pleasure of chauffeuring many famous and well-known individuals. Most of them were wealthy and prominent clients from the community, but on occasion I would be called to drive for some that were famous worldwide.

The limousine company I worked for had a contract for a few years to drive daytime soap stars to and from the airport. They would fly into town to do interviews for a cable show called Soap Scoop. There were two soap stars that I remember from the daytime show All My Children who played the characters Jenny and Jessie. Both were exceptionally nice, which made it a lot of fun. I was able to get autographs from both for my mother, who was the only person I knew at the time that watched them. It was great to watch the shows after chauffeuring them around town.

I also had the pleasure of driving for the rock-n-roll band Rosie on a frigid New Year's Eve. The lead singer, Mark, rented the limo for the entire night, and I sat front and center at the nightclub with the band members' wives and girlfriends. It was a long night filled with celebration, drinking, dancing, and babysitting the drunks in our party. No matter how much you pay for a party dress, throwing up in front of two hundred people sort of blows it. I did, however, leave the after party with a great tip and an album signed by all of the band members.

One of the most unforgettable experiences was driving two very famous gentlemen to dinner. Both have worldwide fame and are extremely wealthy. One is very well known in the sports world, having been an owner of a professional team, and the other is well known in broadcasting.

The evening started out as usual with the Rolls Royce headed to a downtown hotel. As I pulled up to the hotel and walked into the lobby, I immediately recognized both men. There was a man asking for their autographs, and as they finished signing his magazine I introduced myself and asked if they were ready to go to dinner. Both men shook my hand as they introduced themselves to me. With a smile, I responded by saying, "my pleasure to meet you both." Both were very well dressed in meticulously tailored suits that made them look like a million dollars.

We made our way to the Rolls Royce and I opened the back doors for them to get in. I was awestruck as I proceeded to get behind the wheel. As we pulled away, they started talking business, and this was one of those occasions during which I knew not to speak unless spoken to. During these types of conversations, there is a sixth sense that tells you not to interrupt or interject. As a professional chauffeur, you hear as much as a bartender does, and a big part of the job is knowing your place, and I knew mine.

We headed to the freeway, as they had reservations at one of our finer restaurants in the northwest part of town. This restaurant used to be a church; it had been beautifully remodeled and was not cheap. A couple could easily spend two to three hundred dollars for dinner there. This was all they wanted to do that evening. I was to drop them off at the restaurant and come back three hours later to take them back to their hotel.

As we headed along the freeway, we passed several points that were familiar to them. One in particular was our university's horseshoe stadium, which they both seemed excited to see in person rather than on TV. One of them asked if I was a fan, and of course I took my chance to pipe in by saying, "absolutely, a die-hard fan." The other gentleman mentioned that the team hadn't done so well during this particular football season, as they were heading to the Liberty Bowl. I said, "yes, but the Liberty Bowl is better than not going to one at all." They both laughed and agreed.

We soon arrived at the restaurant, and as we pulled into the parking lot, I spoke up and reiterated to them the time that they wanted me to return. One of them quickly said, "Ric, you can come in and join us if you want. We're just going to talk business, and you're welcome; we'll buy you dinner or drinks." The other agreed and also asked me to come in with them. I told them that I didn't want to barge in, and they both responded by telling me that I wouldn't be intruding. So I thanked them and said that I would come in after I parked the car in a safe spot. I dropped them off at the door and told them I would see them shortly. After finding a safe spot in the parking lot, I headed in to the restaurant. The hostess stopped me at the door and asked if she could help me. I told her who I was looking for and she pointed out their table.

As I approached the table, I noticed they were drinking and having appetizers. One of them pulled out a chair for me as I got closer to the table. I thanked him, and they resumed talking about sports and various sports figures. They asked if I wanted a drink, and I accepted graciously. As the waiter brought my drink, we were talking, and at this point I was feeling very comfortable with sitting and conversing with them. They were two very nice gentlemen who were confident in their opinions. Their dinners came shortly after my second drink, and their conversation began to loosen as they proceeded to talk about all kinds of sports figures. They talked about whom they liked and didn't like, and then the topic switched to whom they thought and had heard was gay. I almost choked on my Scotch, and I had to grab my napkin to wipe away what didn't make it down my throat after almost spitting it all over the table. I couldn't believe what I was hearing, and they backed up their claims by saying who had actually told them. These two were well connected in the sports world, and I have no doubt about the truth of what they were saying. One of the guys followed this with a comment that I will never forget. He said, "you know, there isn't an industry or a team that doesn't have a gay person on it, and there's nothing wrong with it, they're great players." The other gentlemen responded by saying, "oh, I have no doubt and I agree." As I remained silent, just soaking in the conversation, they looked at me as if to ask my opinion. My only response was, "sure, I'll have another drink." They both burst out laughing, and there we were, almost making spectacles of ourselves in that fine restaurant.

We sat there as they finished their dinners and ordered another round of drinks, and then one of the guys asked the waiter for a phone (this being the time period before everyone carried a cell phone). The phone arrived at the table within minutes, and one of them picked it up and started dialing. The other guy asked, "who are you calling?" "Kosel," he said. "what they hell are you calling him for?" the other guy asked. He replied by saying, "he owes me tickets."

I was again awestruck; this guy was calling Howard Kosel from the table I was sitting at. Howard Kosel was a famous sportscaster who usually covered boxing but also commentated other sporting events and was well connected to these two gentlemen. When Howard answered, one of the gentlemen asked where his tickets were and then laughed. Kosel knew exactly who was calling and said that the tickets were being left at the ticket booth with his name on them. The man with the phone also asked Howard who he thought was going to win the Rose Bowl that year. Howard said that he had put his money on the team from California. After the conversation was over, I could tell they were getting ready for their check. I told them that I would be waiting with the car at the door and advised them to take their time. They asked the waiter for their check, and I headed out to the Rolls. I waited for about ten minutes, and then the restaurant doors opened. I opened both of the back doors for them as they approached. When they were in, I closed the doors, got behind the wheel, and started the car, and we headed back to the hotel downtown. They both mentioned how much fun they had had and how good the dinner had been as I thanked them for buying drinks for me. They continued to talk about sports, and we soon arrived at their hotel. I pulled up, and the doorman opened one of the back doors as I opened the other. When they got out, I shook their hands and thanked them again for the fun evening. As one of the gentlemen shook my hand, he handed me an envelope. I didn't look in it, but quickly put it in the inside pocket of my jacket and said "Thank you!" Inside the envelope was a fifty-dollar tip. What a fun night!

MY FIRST WEDDING

Soon after Ed offered the job to me and we discussed the hourly rate, I received my first call to drive for a wedding. He gave me every detail about the driving job for that next Saturday evening. It was going to be a wedding at the conservatory, and the reception was to be at an old supper club that had been popular in the 1940s and 1950s. It was *the* place to go for dancing to big bands and seeing floorshows. In those times people really dressed up for dinner and an evening out. Now the hall is only rented for private parties.

Ed mentioned that the wedding was at 7:00 p.m., which meant I needed to pick up the car at least thirty minutes beforehand. The bride and groom were having a small wedding with maybe sixty guests. As I arrived, I noticed crowds of three and four people gathering in the parking lot in different spots. Well, I stopped the show when I pulled up in the big Rolls Royce like a cruise ship gracefully moving through the parking lot. I enjoyed driving up slowly; it gave the car a grand entrance. That was the fun part of driving that car. Everyone—and I mean everyone—stopped and looked at it, and what an awesome sight it was. I pulled up to the front of the conservatory, parking right in front, where a limo should. My early arrival gave me time to set up the champagne stand with the glasses and put the "Just Married" sign on the back of the car. That alone was entertainment for some; the sign, the champagne, and the chauffeur standing there in a tuxedo made for a great show. It was a very impressive presentation. While I was standing by the car, smoking a cigarette, two women came up to the car and were admiring it. They were probably in their mid-twenties, and they were very good looking; neither of them was wearing a wedding ring. One of several pieces of advice that Ed gave to me was to be aware of my surroundings while driving and to know what's going on. He said that it's very easy to get into strange situations when driving a limo, especially a Rolls Royce. There are all types of people out there, and I just had to be careful. He said the car would attract everyone, and he was right. His last words were, “don’t set yourself up.”

The two young ladies just wanted to sit in the back seat of the Rolls. Ed mentioned that it would happen and that it would be great public relations to let people sit in the car as long as it didn’t interfere with the paying customer. So I pretty much let anyone do it. For most people it would be their only opportunity to sit in a Rolls Royce, let alone a limousine. There were a few times that I refused to let people sit in the car, and there were obvious reasons I did so. On two occasions it turned ugly, almost breaking into a fistfight, but I can take care of myself.

After trying all of the buttons and gadgets in the back seat, the two ladies started talking about their boyfriends, giving graphic descriptions that would make most people blush. I thought to myself, *they’ve got to know I can hear them.* But they went on commenting on how lucky they were to have boyfriends that got along with each other so well. One of the women mentioned that she thought the guys played golf and went hunting too much with their buddies, but that was about all she said. Soon after this, two men came out of the conservatory and noticed the two women in the back seat. One of the women said, “oh, here are the boys, let’s go." The women quickly opened the doors and got out of the limo. The four of them stood around for a while, looking at the car, chatting, and asking questions that I would become more familiar with as I drove more. I would always be asked if I liked driving the limo, if I made a lot of money, and if it was easy to drive a car with the steering wheel on the right side. I always answered; "yes, it's a lot of fun, the money is good, and driving a right-hand drive car is easier than one would think." That's when the women decided to go in the conservatory to find a seat for the ceremony. The guys said they would be in shortly, and they headed toward the parking lot. As they walked away, they both looked back at the car. I couldn't figure out what they were doing or thinking, but they were obviously up to something. They walked toward one of the cars in the parking lot and got in the front seat. I stood by the Rolls, remembering what Ed had told me, I acted as though I wasn't paying any attention to them, but I actually was. Pretty soon it was obvious what they were up to. They were smoking pot, and I just chuckled. After a few minutes I looked over, and I could see that the driver was bent over with his head down. As I continued to watch, I saw the guy in the passenger seat do the same thing. It was obvious that they were doing coke, and I don't mean the soft drink. This went on for about fifteen minutes, and they got out of the car, wiping their noses and sniffling as they headed toward the conservatory. As they walked by me, one of them snickered, and I could tell they knew what I saw, so I said, "feeling better?" They both busted out laughing, saying yes, and they continued toward the conservatory.

The boys made it in just in time for the ceremony to end. Shortly after they entered, groups of people were starting to exit. It was over, and the guests were heading to their cars. Some were walking over to the limo, where I had positioned myself for the bride and groom. There were a few people waiting to pelt them with birdseed. As I was standing there in my tux, I looked around and saw the two guys that had been in the car. They both were standing there holding their girlfriend's hands, just stoned. At that point I couldn't do anything but laugh to myself. Ed had said that I was going to see all kinds of situations, and he was right.

As the bride and groom came running out of the conservatory toward the Rolls, they tried to shield themselves from the birdseed, but were pelted from all directions. When they got to the car, I popped the cork and started pouring the champagne into their glasses. They were glowing with joy and having a great time. We all stood there for a few minutes as everyone clicked their cameras, catching the photo opportunity. After they toasted each other and kissed, with the crowd applauding, I helped the bride get her dress into the back seat. The groom got in the door on the opposite side as I placed the champagne bucket by his feet. With cameras clicking, I got behind the wheel and started the engine, and then we drove off. They wanted to go around the block so people would leave and they could then go back in and take pictures. They were kissing and drinking and pawing each other in the back seat and I thought to myself, *these two are not going to be able to make it through the reception.* They calmed down as we pulled back into the parking lot of the conservatory, as most of the guests' cars were gone. I got out to open the car door for them as they headed in for pictures. After about thirty minutes, they were heading back to the car. As they approached, I got out to let them in. They both were very nice, and they thanked me for waiting and opening the doors. I got behind the wheel, started the engine, and began to pull away. Not long afterward, I heard the groom whispering. I thought something was coming, and I was right; just then the bride spoke up and asked if I minded if they did some cocaine. Well, I was shocked at the forwardness, but I said, "Feel free to do whatever you two want; it's your day. But be discreet; we don't want to advertise, now do we?" They responded with a no and began to satisfy their urge.

I really didn't mind, since I knew I was in control and I wanted my customers to be comfortable while riding with me. That was when I heard the groom say, "Would you like to do some?" I responded by saying, "no, one of us has to keep it together." They laughed and got a kick out of my comment, but they understood. The reception hall was about a twenty-five minute drive from the conservatory, and we had about twenty minutes to go when I heard some noises coming from the back seat. Bingo! They were going at it—having sex! I was so embarrassed that I wanted to crawl under the front seat, but I just turned up the volume on the stereo and tilted the rearview mirror to give them some privacy. There was no glass divider between the driver and passengers, nor were the windows tinted, as you see with most limousines. Every car that passed us could see what was going on, and every one of them laid on the horn. I calmly looked at each car that passed and smiled and waved. I never realized just how much space actually was in that back seat but apparently it was more than enough. How she did it in that dress was beyond me. As we approached the reception hall, they both thanked me again as they were frantically trying to put themselves back together and hide the guilt on their faces. We pulled into the parking lot of the reception hall with about fifteen minutes left on the time remaining that they had rented the car for, so they asked if the bride's grandmother could sit in the car. I said, "sure, no problem." I let them out, leaving the doors open to air out the car, and then I went to the trunk to get the leather cleaner.

I wanted to be sure that grandma didn't get her dress messy or ask about any odors. Grandma soon came out, and I said, "let's go!"

This lady was very excited to be in the Rolls, and she was making me crazy. If only she had known what had just gone on in the back seat, she would have died. We drove around the block, and then I had to take her back. I pulled back into the reception hall parking lot and stopped in front of the door. I got out and opened the door for her and helped her to the entrance. Just about that time, I noticed the groom was coming out and walking toward me; he had an envelope in his hand, which I was hoping was for me. He handed me the envelope and said, as we were shaking hands, "thank you for everything; I mean everything.". I thanked him and gave him my business card, telling him to call if they ever needed a driver. He said he would and thanked me again as he went back into the reception. I went to the Rolls, got in, and headed back to the garage.

This was my first wedding and my first experience in a situation like this. I remembered what Ed had said about keeping the car clean, but I hadn't banked on sex. I soon began to expect it, however, as it happened often.

Being the good chauffeur I wanted to be, I often wondered if I should keep an assortment of condoms in the glove box just in case.

Exposure to all types and kinds of people was what I was in for, and I was having the time of my life. I was also enjoying the tips. It was not a bad deal as long as the extracurricular activity didn't get out of hand.

THE LEPRE-CONS

Several months had passed, and by this time I was really enjoying this job. This particular day started as usual while I was working at the law firm. I never knew when Ed would call and ask me to drive, but it was usually when he couldn't do it. He, too, enjoyed the money, and if he drove, he also received the tips.

The phone rang, and it was Ed calling to confirm a booking. It was St. Patrick's Day, and it was going to be a strange evening; I could just feel it. I never enjoyed being out with the drinking amateurs driving and clogging the highways on this holiday. St. Patrick's Day is just as bad as New Year's Eve for drunks on the road. It seemed to be one of those holidays that some people consider an open invitation to drink and drive and act as stupidly as they can. This was also a time when drinking and driving laws were not as strict as they are currently. Now when you drink and drive and get caught, you're in for a long stay and a hefty fine. But being a chauffeur is good money, and it can be fun to watch the customers cut loose, as long as it's not too loose. By this time I had experienced quite a bit while driving for the public, but just when I thought I had seen it all, I quickly realized I was wrong. This particular booking was scheduled for me to pick up two men at a downtown hotel around 7:30 p.m. They wanted a night out on the town, as they were from a small southern town and they had come to our city to have some fun. To top it off, they wanted to go to a nightclub that was an internationally known chain at which the cocktail waitresses wore seductive attire.

The club had only been open for about six months, and it wasn't doing very well from what I heard. The major problem was the location. It was on the east side of town by a shopping mall. This was not a good business move, as this place should have been downtown by the hotels, where they would get customers that didn't have to drive or take a cab to get to it. The chances of it being successful would have been a lot better if it had been there. I was excited about the booking and was looking forward to it, knowing that I was often invited in with customers at restaurants. Prior to leaving the garage with the Rolls, I always gathered plenty of iced champagne bottles and several glasses and then cleaned the back seat and windows. As I never knew who had been in the car prior to me, I always made sure the car was clean and prepped. The next stop was a fill up at the gas station.

I was prompt that evening, picking up the customers by 7:30 p.m. as planned. I pulled up in front of the hotel and went to the front desk to have the clerk contact the guests in their room. The clerk pointed to two gentlemen sitting in the bar, drinking. He wanted me to go to the bar myself to tell them that the limo was there waiting for them. I thought it was strange, but I didn't think much about it at the time. Little did I know that the hotel staff had already had enough of these two gentlemen. So I walked toward the bar, and as I got closer to them I realized why the desk clerk wanted me to see them for myself.

The two were wearing polyester leisure suits with wide lapels. To put the finishing touches on their outfits, they both wore cowboy boots and had their hair all greased back. What a sight! I hadn't seen a leisure suit for at least twenty years, and the sad part was that they thought they were all decked out and looking cool and ready to paint the town. I couldn't help myself, and I started laughing without them seeing me. I was thinking to myself, *here I am driving Gomer and Goober from Mayberry out on a date.* I quickly stopped laughing when I was hit with the reality that I would be spending several hours with them. Here's this beautiful Rolls Royce, me in a tuxedo and driving cap, them in the back seat all dressed up, and we were going to dinner. This was going to be a priceless evening.

I introduced myself to them and said, "Gentlemen, I'll be waiting at the car while you clear your tab." It was about five minutes later when they came out to the Rolls. They got in the back seat, and I shut the doors for them as usual. I looked back toward the lobby as we pulled away just in time to see a few of the employees gathered in the lobby, laughing. But all I do is drive the Rolls; how difficult could the evening be? Right? Wrong. Oh, so wrong.

So we pulled away from the hotel and headed toward the club. As we were driving along, they were in the back seat just hee-hawing away. They were talking about the sexy waitresses they were going to meet, and saying they were going to, as they put it, "get them some women and drive them around in the big car." They were also raving about the car and about their looking really rich. To this day I'm not even sure if they knew it was a Rolls Royce. I told them to let me open and close the doors for them when we arrived at the restaurant. They said, "All right, that would look real good." Well, I knew I was in for a treat, especially since I had to tell them that I would get the doors for them.

We arrived at the club, and there were some other people going in as we pulled up to the door. I stopped the car, turned off the ignition, got out, and opened the doors to let them out. Everyone within eyeshot stopped what they were doing and just looked at us with amazement. I asked how long they would be since I would be waiting outside for them. One of the guys answered in a deep, deep southern drawl and said, "why son, I think we might be here a spell, so why don't you come on in and join us?" Usually, I'd rather tend to the car so no one would bother it, but this was an event I couldn't pass up. I said, "Okay I'll be right in after I park the car." They headed in, and I parked the car in a spot where it could be seen from the front desk of the club. I asked the receptionist to keep an eye on the car, and he said he would. I headed down the long hallway to the restaurant and noticed that the two gentlemen were sitting just inside the doorway. It was an odd table, but I think they had been a little nervous and had sat down at the first table they saw. They were very happy to see me, because my appearance told everyone that they had a driver for the night. They ordered drinks and offered me a Scotch and water. After about ten minutes I couldn't stand it any longer, so I told them they would be more successful in picking up women if I weren't sitting with them. I told them that I would be sitting at the bar, mostly because I didn't want any part of whatever they were up to. So I walked over to the bar, pulled up a stool, and sat back to watch the show with the bartender. What a show it was, too.

They hit on every waitress that walked by their table. They were even staring at a woman that was at the next table with her husband. These guys obviously hadn't been in the company of a lady for a while. Nor had they been in public, which was apparent by the way they were acting; they had no social skills at all. I thought I was with two squirrels chasing a nut. I sat at the bar, cracking up laughing at them making fools of themselves and drinking Scotch on their tab.

They sat at their table and had drinks and dinner as I watched from the bar. I noticed they were talking about something and looking at me. I was petrified, not knowing what was coming when one of the guys came over and asked if I'd like to have my picture taken with some of the waitresses. I agreed to the picture, as I needed some type of proof of the evening. Plus, I knew that if I had a picture of these guys, it would be easier for everyone to believe me.

We went over to the stairway where the pictures were being taken. First they each took a picture, and then they motioned for me to come over. As I approached them, I could hear what they were saying. One of them was telling the waitresses about how rich they were. He said that they were in the oil business and had recently sold a rig, and he even pulled a check out of his wallet for twenty-seven thousand dollars, trying to impress everyone. After I had my picture taken with the waitresses, we headed back to the dinning room.

As we were walking back to our seats, I heard one of the guys talking to a waitress about coming back to the hotel with them. She kept insisting that they were not allowed to do that. But the guys kept insisting that they could if they just didn't tell anyone about it. Well, this unconvincing act went on for a couple of hours. Closing time was 2:30 a.m. so I knew—or thought—that the evening would be ending soon and that I could go home and end this pain. I walked over to their table, informed them of the time, and told them that I was going to pull the car around to the front door and wait for them. One of them thought that was a good idea. He turned to the waitress he had been talking to and said, "now you just go find a friend to come back to the hotel with us, and I'll give you each another hundred dollars."

As I found out later, he had already given her two hundred dollars to split with her friend, and they each would get another hundred for coming back to the hotel. I couldn't believe my ears as I headed to get the car. Well, I stood by the car for another half hour, and the two finally came out. Like I had expected, they were alone. I couldn't wait to hear this, so I opened the doors and let them in the back seat, shut their doors, and got behind the wheel. As I started the car and began to pull away a voice came from the back seat, saying, "stop, we're waiting for our dates. They said they would be right out." I said okay, put the car in park, and we sat there. We waited and waited, but no one came out of the front door. By this time there were no other customers in sight. I noticed that there were only two other cars in the parking lot, and it was getting close to 3:00 a.m. We sat there waiting for the waitresses until 3:30 a.m.—one whole hour after they walked out. As you've already guessed by now, those waitresses never came out. They had slipped out the back door and gone home to their families. I asked the guys if it was all right to leave and head back or if they wanted to stay and wait a little longer.

They realized that they had been jilted, and they were mad as hell about losing the money. One got out of the car and walked up to the front door of the club and started pounding on the door. I laughed to myself as the other still sat in the back seat. The guy pounding on the door got back in the car and was really pissed off by that time. He said, "that bitch took my money; I want some action." He then said, "let's get out of here and find us something." That something turned out to be prostitutes. We were driving toward downtown when one guy asked if I knew where they could get a couple of girls for the night. I told them that I didn't know. They didn't believe me, and playing to my vanity they kept insisting that a good-looking stud like me must know where to find women—lots of women. I told them that I was sorry but that I couldn't help them. I did suggest that someone at their hotel might be able to help them find women, but the sight of these guys made me ill. I just wanted to dump them back at their hotel and be done with it.

By the time we arrived back at the hotel, they were even more upset. I guess since they had spent over five hundred dollars for dinner with just each other and ended up with only each other to go home with, they took their frustration out on me. As we approached the hotel, they started making comments about the limo service and how the service was bad. At least that's the way they saw it, but I was not going to drive that Rolls Royce into some questionable part of town to track down some skanky prostitutes for them. I drove for them from 7:00 p.m. to 4:00 a.m., which is nine hours, and needless to say, I received no tip; only a picture of myself with the waitresses at the club. I had known that those waitresses were taking their money, but these men were too stupid to realize that they were being taken to the cleaners.

So I opened the doors for them to get out, and they were so mad at me that they didn't even say thanks or goodbye, so I knew for sure no tip was coming. I wasn't mad about the way they treated me because I had come to expect it from certain customers. Tip or no tip, I was just glad to be rid of them and on my way home. When I arrived at the garage, I pulled in and began to clean up the car for the next job.

I finished cleaning up the car and locked the garage doors and began walking to the house to wash the champagne glasses. Yes, I had to do all of that too. I took my time, racking up the hours to make up for not getting an increase in my hourly rate. For what I was doing, five dollars an hour was lower than the industry standard. It wasn't a bad job as long as people tipped properly.

As I entered the back door of the house, Ed's fiancée greeted me, saying that the guys had called expressing their disappointment in our ability to provide good service. I explained to her that it meant I wouldn't drive around to find them a prostitute. They also said that I had kept their pictures of them with the waitresses and that they wanted them back. She was laughing, but she agreed that I had done the right thing and asked if I would take the pictures to the hotel. I had already put the Rolls away, so I decided to drive my car. So, wearing my tux, I jumped in my old beat-up Duster and headed downtown. I was hoping not to see either one of those greaseballs ever again, but it looked like I would.

I pulled up in front of the hotel, and I noticed that the only person around was the lobby desk clerk, who was different from the clerk I had seen earlier.

I gave him their names and room number for him to call, and I explained the situation.

He looked at me and smiled and said, “I know. They called the front desk several times asking me to look out for you and insisting that you bring the pictures up to their room.” I looked back at the desk clerk and said, “there is no way in hell I’m going up to that room; you can if you want. Besides, I have seen the movie Deliverance; have you?” He said, “I gotcha, I’ll have them come down, thank you very much.” I turned around and walked out of the hotel lobby to get back in my car and go home.

Every St. Patrick’s Day since, I chuckle to myself as I think about driving those two yahoos, and I am very thankful for avoiding a potentially dangerous ending to that evening.

THE BIRTHDAY SURPRISE

It was a cold and blustery December evening for this driving job. Everyone was in the holiday spirit; parties were everywhere. Our client had planned a surprise birthday celebration for his wife but told her it was a Christmas party. Their home was in a small town about forty miles outside of the city. The job would require two cars to drive guests to and from the house: our Silver Cloud II and another Rolls Royce that we leased on an as-needed basis. The owner lived in a beautiful home that was probably in the million–dollar-plus range with his wife and their six children, and he was in dire need of a maid. The house was always a wreck.

I was driving the second Rolls Royce that evening, so I headed out of town to the party, which took almost an hour to get to. The best route to take was a two-lane highway, and I never liked driving that stretch of road because traffic was fast and there was always someone behind you impatiently wanting to pass. This is what happened that night as I was on my way to this job. I was driving the speed limit with one car behind me when I noticed a line of cars and trucks approaching as normal. Suddenly, I noticed headlights that seemed to be coming directly at me in my lane. That's when it became clear; that car was headed directly for me. It was passing on a double yellow line and approaching fast at about sixty miles per hour. I had no time to think; all I knew was that I needed to get out of their way, and there was nowhere to go except off of the road. There was about five inches of snow just at the edge of the road, so I knew I couldn't take all four wheels into the snow. I had to keep two wheels on dry pavement; if that Rolls went off the road completely, there would be no coming back. With the two right wheels off of the road and in the snow, the Rolls was traveling along just as the car coming at me blew past, missing the car behind me by inches. I had about five seconds to react, and I got over just in time. The Rolls fishtailed in the snow, and I barely maintained control as I slowly brought it back onto the highway. Once I was back on dry pavement, I found an area where I could pull off and calm down. My heart was pounding, and after a few minutes I was able to continue on, and I arrived at the party in plenty of time.

The house was about a half mile into the woods. We were hired to drive the guests to the house after they parked their cars by the street. With two cars, walkie-talkies were a must, since the driveway was only one lane and we each needed to know where the other was. The guests were dressed to the max, and I had never seen so many mink coats in my life. For the next ninety minutes, we drove guests from their cars to the house. Everyone was in a cheerful mood and feeling special as the Rolls Royces shuttled them. Every guest also brought a gift for the wife who was turning fifty.

After the initial rush of guests arriving, the other driver and I decided it would be a good idea for one of us to be up at the house in case someone wanted to leave. I was the driver at the house when some of the guests came out to look over the Rolls Royce. They always have the same questions. "What's it like to drive on the wrong side of the car?" I always responded that it was the right side, not the wrong side. That always generated a laugh, and there was always the smart one that would say, "I think it's illegal to have one of those cars in the United States, isn't it?" I always answered their questions and comments professionally and with a smile.

After entertaining a few of the guests, I noticed two women coming out to the car. They introduced themselves; one of them was the birthday girl. The other was introduced as her best friend. We had been talking for about a half hour when the husband of the birthday girl joined us. He handed me an envelope that turned out to be my tip. I got a fifty-dollar tip for the five hours I had been there. *Not bad,* I thought. Then someone yelled from the house for the birthday girl to come to the phone. She went in, leaving her husband and her best friend talking to me. We talked for a few minutes, and then the husband wanted to go for a ride in the Rolls. He asked his wife's best friend if she wanted to tag along. She agreed.

I quickly opened the doors for them and contacted the other driver to let him know I was taking them for a ride and to ask him to come up to the house in case anyone else wanted to leave. As soon as the other driver came up to the house, we headed down the driveway. After a few minutes with the husband and the wife's best friend in the car, I realized why I had received a tip in advance. Before we were even out of the driveway, I began to hear kissing in the back seat. I looked in the rearview mirror and saw that the best friend had a lip lock on the husband. I heard his belt buckle come undone, and the next thing I knew, bingo! they were going at it as if I was not even in the car. This went on for about ten minutes as I kept turning the volume up on the stereo. Initially I had Christmas music playing, but I quickly changed the station; "The Twelve Days of Christmas" was a bit inappropriate, as all I could hear was, "my true love gave to me."

Shortly after, the husband asked me to take them back to the house, which I did. I guess there is still one surprise for his wife.

When they went into the house, I radioed the other driver and told him to stay where he was. I was on my way to talk to him. It wasn't funny, but all we could do was laugh.

The rest of the night went as planned, driving the guests from the house to their cars, and after a while the husband came out to tell us we could leave. He first walked over to the other driver and shook his hand, and then he came over to me and reached out for my hand. I smiled and extended my hand. As we were shaking hands, he winked at me and said, "thank you for the nice ride." I replied by saying, "thank you sir, but I didn't give you the ride."

He just burst out laughing, and then I felt him handing me money as we were shaking hands. I discretely put it in my pocket to look at later. I guess this was hush money. After all of the guests had been taken to their cars, we left for home. On the way home, I looked at the tip. He had given me another fifty-dollar bill.

DRIVING THE COUNTESS

I thought I had made it to the big time when Ed told me about this particular booking. I was to pick up a famous French Countess from a posh condo on the near east side of midtown and drive her and her escort to the opera.

I didn't follow opera at the time, but it was a highly publicized production. There were also three big-name celebrities in the lineup, and the advertising had started several months prior, so everyone knew about it.

I picked up the car at Ed's and gathered the champagne, glasses, and napkins to serve with. As usual, I arrived just ahead of the scheduled time and was waiting in front of the building for them to come out. Shortly after I arrived, out came a gorgeous, petite woman and a very handsome African American man. Her full-length gown was strapless, white, and very sleek looking. Her escort wore a perfectly tailored black tuxedo. By her walk, one could tell that she reeked of money, status, and power. She wore a turban with a broach that was loaded with jewels that sparkled with her every move. She was dressed like a million dollars and was very beautiful.

The two of them walked up to the car and said hello as I opened the back door of the limo for them to get in. The gentleman said that they wanted the champagne iced and held until after the opera. He also said that her publicity team would be snapping pictures at the theater. This really added to the glitz, and I really felt like I was driving royalty. They settled into the back seat, and then I got behind the wheel and started to drive off. The Countess spoke French, which I didn't understand. I looked at the gentleman, and he then translated. She asked for classical music on the stereo, and I quickly changed the station. The two of them spoke French, and it appeared as though he was giving a tour, explaining various buildings along the way. As we pulled up to the curb in front of the theater, I noticed that several men with cameras were waiting out front. Well, when we pulled up in the huge Rolls Royce, we stopped everyone dead in their tracks. I stopped directly in front of the theater and got out to open the doors for them as the crowd was mumbling and flash bulbs were going off left and right. It really felt like a Hollywood premier. Those in line to buy tickets stopped in their tracks, watching to see who was in the car. I closed the door to the Rolls as they headed to the entrance, pausing occasionally for pictures. One person even asked for her autograph, which she very gracefully gave. Then they headed in to find their seats.

It was a beautiful evening. There was a clear sky, and it was a midsummer seventy-five degrees. The Rolls was spotless, and all was going well. It was a night to remember. This type of driving job is a lot of fun, and I enjoyed playing my part.

The opera would last about two hours, and the wait was the part of the driving job I also enjoyed. I would visit friends and drive them to get ice cream or go through a fast food drive through window. I knew that on this particular evening, I would have at least two hours before I had to return to pick my customers up.

I arrived back at the theater and asked one of the ushers how much longer the opera would be. She said it would be ending soon. It would have been a disaster to have them come out of the theater with me not waiting there for them.

I was enjoying this evening; I felt like Max on the television show *Hart to Hart*. I always thought Max had a great job.

I was suddenly brought to attention when I noticed that people were exiting the theater. The Countess obviously had front row seats; she and the gentleman with her were practically the last ones out of the theater, which was the plan so the media would be in place.

By the time they came out, a large crowd had gathered by the Rolls to see who was going to get in. I had mentioned to a few curious onlookers that it was a Countess from France and her escort. I looked up, and there they were, heading right for the Rolls. The crowd began to applaud as they got in the back seat of the Rolls, and then I closed the doors and got in, and we drove away from the cheering crowd with cameras clicking.

We were about one block away when I suddenly heard the voices of two *men* in the back seat. I looked in the rearview mirror and almost wrecked the car. The Countess was a man! He was a drag queen who was now speaking perfect English; I had been totally fooled. It was the perfect scam, as no one in the theater knew. I know that because if it had been found out, they would have been harassed to the point of having to leave the theater.

It turned out that this drag queen had hired all of the people taking pictures, and the escort was his boyfriend. They were also having a party at their condo, and they asked me to join them for a drink. I couldn't stand not going, so I returned the Rolls to the garage and then went back for the party. When I returned, they were very happy to see me. I met all of their friends that night, and we had a great time laughing about the evening.

Oh, and one more piece unfolded weeks after the scam. There was an article in the section of the paper called "Letters to the Editor." In it was a letter from the Countess mentioning that our town was on the map. I read it and just laughed and read on. The drag queen also thanked the city in the letter. Apparently, he sent the letter to a friend in Paris and had that friend add postage to it and mail it back to the paper. In that letter, the Countess just raved about our city and how beautiful the theater was.

It was the biggest scam; I couldn't believe that this conservative, hometown newspaper didn't even check her out first.

Instead, they fell for it hook, line, and sinker.

TRICK-OR-TREAT

It was a Tuesday evening in late October as we were painting the living room in our apartment while listening to classical music. It was about 7:30 p.m. when the phone rang; it was Ed wanting to know if I could do a job that evening. He said that a friend of his wife from high school was in town and wanted to rent the Rolls. The only stipulation was that the car had to be at his hotel by 8:30 p.m. or he would call another limo service. Ed stated that they guy would be paying cash up front for three hours, plus a tip. He then added that the client may want to rent the limo for more than the three hours by extending the evening and paying cash and tipping for the additional hours and champagne as he requested them.

Well, I decided to do the job and began to move quickly. I jumped in the shower and was soon on my way. I arrived at the garage at 8:20, and Ed had the Rolls engine running for me, and he had also filled the tank and stocked the car with champagne and glasses.

I quickly got in the Rolls and drove toward the hotel, making it there right at 8:30 p.m. I went to the front desk and asked the clerk to contact the clients to let them know I was there and waiting. I returned to the car to set up the champagne and glasses while waiting for my clients to come out.

After ten minutes or so, they came to the car. The gentleman paying was named Don. He walked through the door and introduced himself to me. His date, Jeannie, appeared as though she was ready to go bowling. She had on ratty blue jeans, a denim jacket, and a tube top. Her shoes were worn out and falling apart. It was safe to say that he really did just pick her up off of the street corner. Which one I have no idea, but I knew I was in store for another weird night; I could just tell.

I served the champagne and felt as though I had two kids in the back seat. These two were so out of place sitting in the Rolls Royce and drinking champagne that I had to chuckle to myself. After the glasses were full, I placed the champagne carrier near Don so he could do the honors and fill the glasses while I was driving, which was normal.

We had just pulled out of the parking lot of the hotel when Don spoke up and said that he and Jeannie would like to do some shopping. I said, "great, where would you like to go?" Don looked at Jeannie, and she mentioned the name of a particularly large department store. I said, "we'll be there in a few minutes."

Don thanked me as he handed me the money for the evening, not including any additional hours or champagne. He gave me a ninety-dollar tip up front and at that point became my new best friend. You could say that the three of us bonded immediately. Money is good! Also, by this time I had seen and heard plenty in the back seat of that car, so there wasn't anything that they could do to shock me. But I've said that before, too.

As we approached the department store, Don spoke up and said, "we'll be in the store for a while, so could you please clean the windows?" I said, "Yes sir." But what a jerk! The windows had been clean when I picked them up; he had deliberately put his handprint on the glass. I stopped the car front of the store, got out, and opened the door for them to get out. I secured the champagne and pulled the car around to the parking lot to clean the windows. They were all clean except for his handprint.

You know, I had been driving for quite a while by that point, and I was beginning to notice a nasty pattern in some people. I straightened up the back seat and gave them clean glasses. Don also had requested that I be back at a certain time to pick them up.

I arrived at his designated time, and they soon came out. My mouth dropped to the ground; I could not believe my eyes. The woman had a new outfit, a new hairstyle, and new boots. Her slacks and waist-length jacket were made of black silk, and her blouse was white with ruffles on the front. The boots, of course, were black too. She had also done something with her hair, as it was pulled back and pinned up in a sophisticated style, unlike it had been an hour earlier. Don had on the same suit as before, but he looked fine the way he was. I opened the doors for them, filled their glasses with champagne, and then closed the doors. Don had a bag to put in the trunk, which he said was filled with her old clothes. I put the bag in the trunk, and we pulled away as I complimented her on the new outfit. She said that it was beautiful and that Don had bought it for her. The next thing I heard coming from the back seat was the sound of a zipper. You guessed it! There they were going at it. I realized at that point that Don had found a hooker at the hotel bar. She did look good in that outfit, but as soon as she opened her mouth it was obvious she was a real airhead.

I quickly realized that she was drugged up on something. They didn't do any in the car; I think they did it in the store. I just kept an eye on her while she tripped out for a few minutes. Since Don was paying for the open hours of driving, I asked if there was any particular place they wanted to go. He said, "I know where I want to go and I'll tell you; just drive." I never acknowledged that he even made a comment. I just thought to myself, *you dick!* Well, after ten minutes of driving with no direction, he decided to tell me where they wanted to go. I wasn't going to say another word.

Don asked me to take them to a small suburb, and he specifically told me which roads to take. We were just about as far into the country as you could get when he said to turn left at the next road. This took us down a long, dark back road.

I suddenly heard Ed's voice telling me to be aware of my surroundings in the Rolls and not to let someone take advantage of me. This kept running through my mind, and it was making me nervous when Don interrupted my train of thought by asking me to turn left into a driveway just ahead. It was a dirt driveway, and it was very dark out in the countryside. I said, "are you sure this is a driveway?" Don assured me that this dirt road would lead us to a house. He pointed out a dim light in the distance and mentioned that it was a floodlight on the house. He said a friend he wanted to visit lived there, but I didn't believe him. I actually thought they were taking me out into the dark night to kill me. I was already creeped out, and I thought it was the end for me. I just had a strange feeling about the area.

As we got closer to the light, I realized that Don was right. It was a floodlight on a house—a very bright floodlight. That surprised me, as did the mile-long driveway. I can't tell you what was going through my mind as I drove down that driveway, but my heart was pounding with fear.

If I would not have had to give so much money back to him, I would have considered leaving them and getting the hell out of that place while I was still alive. The two of them got out of the car and walked up to the house and knocked on the door. There I was, standing next to the car by myself in the dark. My imagination was working overtime as I was really starting to imagine all kinds of things while staring into the darkness in the middle of nowhere. At one point I thought I saw someone in the field next to the house. I stared at that spot for a minute and it moved again. That's when I jumped in the car, started the engine, and locked the doors. I was going to be ready to take off and get away from whatever it was. I could just see Bigfoot coming out of the woods, attacking the car, and pulling me out to eat me. I didn't want to die like that. I turned the car around so that I would be ready to travel down that long, dark, bumpy dirt driveway at a moment's notice toward civilization and safety. While I was sitting in the car, I heard noises that seemed to come from the other side of the car. I thought, *this is it, something or someone is going to jump out at me, it's Bigfoot, I just know it.* I had a feeling of being watched from all directions, but I convinced myself that I was just paranoid. I didn't know what it was, and I didn't want to find out. I did know one thing for sure; I was not unlocking the doors or getting out of that car until someone came out of the house.

It reminded me of scary movies in which someone hears a noise outside and goes out to check it out while in the meantime, the villain is waiting in the dark of night, ready to pounce. Well, that wasn't going to happen to me.

Ten minutes later I noticed that the door to the house started to open. Don and Jeannie then came out and started toward the limo. The person they were visiting never stepped into doorway. I unlocked the doors and got out to open the doors of the Rolls. They got in the back seat; I closed the doors and then got behind the wheel and took off down that dark driveway. I felt like doing it at one hundred miles per hour, but I didn't tell them why, nor did I say anything about the figure in the woods. I knew someone had been watching us, but I just wanted to get out of there, so I didn't say a word. My heart was beating so fast that I was forgetting to breathe.

When we pulled out onto the road I felt much better. Soon we were on the main highway, and within minutes Don mentioned that they wanted to go to a bar on the near west side of town. It was a little dive bar; I was very familiar with the area, having grown up on the west side. This bar was not the type of bar that I wanted to go into. I'll say this much, you could count on a fight breaking out either in the bar or in the parking lot on any given night. It wasn't only the guys, but the women too. The women in this place enjoyed a brawl every now and then. I wanted no part of this place, so I sat in the car while they went in. After all, I had to protect that Rolls.

For some reason, Jeannie came out to the car by herself. I didn't question it, but she did say that

Don would be right out. While we were sitting there, she asked me if I wanted to smoke some pot with her. By this time, I was ready for a smoke to calm me down, but I refused, having the responsibility of the Rolls in my hands. She pulled out a joint and lit it. She took a couple of puffs from it and then put it out. All I needed was for drugs to be in the ashtray.

We were sitting there listening to the stereo when I saw Don come out of the bar. He walked toward the Rolls, so I got out to open his door for him to get in. I opened the second bottle of champagne and again filled their glasses. We sat in the car for a few minutes while they smoked pot and drank their champagne, and then I asked where they wanted to go next. I was almost afraid to ask for fear of them wanting to go to a cockfight or dogfight. That was about the only thing left for them to do that night. After all, my nerves were being put through the wringer already, so nothing would surprise me from that point on.

While they were in the back seat, Don asked Jeannie if she had anyone she wanted to visit. Jeannie said that it would be fun to stop by her mother's house, which was about twenty minutes away. By the time we arrived, they had finished the second bottle of champagne. While inside, I cleaned up the glasses and had another bottle ready to open when they came out.

They had spent about a half-hour in her mom's house when I saw them coming out of the front door. The three of them walked toward the Rolls, and I decided to make this look very good for the mom, so I got out of the car, opened the back door, and stood there like a professional chauffeur would. We all talked for a few minutes; her mother was very nice. They said their goodbyes as Don and Jeannie got back in the Rolls, and I closed the door, asking if they wanted more champagne. Don said, "sure." So I decided to open a new bottle of champagne while I was sitting in the front seat. I tore off the foil wrapper and started twisting the cork, and then it happened—a chauffeur's worst nightmare. That cork blew out of the top of that bottle like a bullet. It bounced all over the interior of the car then *pow!* It hit Don square in the eye. I couldn't have planned it better myself. I quietly laughed and thought, "that will teach you to mess up my clean windows!"

After we realized that he was all right, all three of us just started laughing hysterically. They had smoked some pot, and they just couldn't stop laughing when I asked where they would like to go next. That seemed to be the question of the night.

Every time I asked that question, we headed to another questionable part of town.

Don reminded me that the time already paid for was about to end. He wanted to pay for an additional two hours, which was ninety dollars. He also wanted another bottle of champagne, which would make their fourth bottle, and it was another five bucks. He gave me an additional $150.00 for the extra time and bottle. That meant that the extra fifty-five dollars was my tip. I had no problem with that, although I did have to go to work the next day, but it was turning out to be a profitable night, and I was in it for the long haul.

Don mentioned a restaurant/bar on the northwest side of town that he wanted to go to. He said that a friend of his owned it, and after that tip, I quickly headed in that direction. I had been to this place several times; it was a great place to meet people, and it had good food.

We arrived at approximately 1:00 a.m., and I pulled up in front of the bar, got out, and opened the door to let them out. Don and Jeannie headed in as I parked the car in a spot from which I could see the front door so I would be ready to quickly pull up to pick them up.

They had been in the bar for about an hour when I saw them in the doorway with the person

I suspected to be the owner. I quickly pulled up to the door of the bar and got out to let the three of them in the back. Don introduced me to the owner, who was a very nice guy who had the appearance of a gangster. Don said they wanted to get a pizza, so we headed to the pizza place that was a mile away.

When we arrived at the pizza place, Jeannie wanted to stay in the car. I couldn't figure this one out. Don and the owner of the bar went in and ordered pizza. After a few minutes Don came out to the car and insisted that Jeannie come in. She went in, and five minutes later the owner came out to the Rolls by himself. He wanted me to take him back to the bar and then return to pick up Don and Jeannie. I opened the door to the Rolls, he got in, and we headed to the bar.

It took about ten minutes to get there and back. When I pulled up in front of the pizza place, Don and Jeannie were waiting. I guess they were ready to go. They came out to the Rolls, and I opened the door for them to get in the back. By this time it was going on 3:00 a.m., and they both were ready to pass out. Don handed the pizza box to me to put on the floor in the front seat. There wasn't much room in the back with the two of them sprawled out and the champagne carrier on the floor.

Knowing that I had to be at work by 8:00 a.m., I was happy we were headed back to the hotel. It also didn't look like I was going to get much sleep, but I was given a total tip of $145.00. That helped me get over the lack of sleep I was thinking about.

So we headed down the freeway toward the downtown hotel. It wasn't a major chain, but a little raggedy hotel that had been open for years. I noticed that it was about 3:15 a.m. when we arrived at the hotel, and there were no other cars in sight. I looked in the rearview mirror and saw that Don and Jeannie were both asleep. I thought, *gee, I wonder if they would miss a couple of pieces of pizza,* but I resisted and didn't eat any.

The hotel had a one-way driveway that went under part of the building and right up to the front door. I would pull right up, let them out, and be on my way home to get some sleep. I couldn't wait; I was starting to doze off myself.

I pulled into the driveway of the hotel and stopped the car in front of the main entrance leading to the lobby. I turned off the ignition, and the two started to come to life. I said, "We're here." They both moaned, and I could tell they just wanted to go back to sleep. I opened the door to get out and remembered that the pizza was on the floor in the front seat, so I got back in and leaned over to get the pizza box.

As I sat up, I noticed in the rearview mirror that two cars were pulling in behind me. This being a one-lane, one-way drive, I just figured that whoever it was would have to wait. Then I noticed a van pulling up in front of the Rolls, going the wrong way and headed right for the car! I immediately thought that we were being robbed. As I got out of the car with the pizza box in my hand, I heard several people yelling, "Police! Freeze!" I looked and saw that they were yelling at me! They were all in blue jeans and they all had police dog tags hanging from their necks; they had their guns drawn and pointed at me. They kept yelling, "police, put your hands in the air and don't move!" So I dropped the pizza box on the ground and my hands went up in the air as they said, "up against the wall; put your hands on the wall." There were about five undercover police all yelling at the same time. I was about to wet my pants. There I was, spread eagle, my hands on the wall, and two guns pressed against the back of my neck. Two officers searched me from head to toe, grabbing and identifying everything in my pockets as one of the officers kicked my legs farther apart as the other continued searching my body—and I mean all of my body. I was about to have a heart attack, having never been arrested before this, not to mention never having been this thoroughly searched. While they were searching me, I could hear everything that Don and Jeannie were saying.

The police pulled them out of the back seat of the Rolls at gunpoint and put each of them in separate cars. While this was happening, Don kept yelling at Jeannie to not tell the police anything. I couldn't believe what the hell I had gotten in the middle of. I was beginning to think that the $145.00 tip wasn't enough for what this jerk put me through.

I kept asking the police what was going on. They said, "you don't know?" I said, "know what? I'm just the chauffeur." I quickly rattled off the name of the limo company, the owner's name, and the company phone number. "You don't' know this guy?" the police asked. I said, "no I don't; I am a hired chauffeur, what's going on?"

The police informed me that I was driving a wanted fugitive and there was a warrant for his arrest. He was wanted in three states for drug trafficking and was in town to answer a subpoena and was not to go outside of the county. They told me I had driven them out of the county three times. I said, "You mean you guys were following us?" They said, "yes, the entire night, trick or treat." Well, all I could think of was Jeannie smoking pot in the parking lot at that bar while we were being watched the whole time. The police were trying to catch Don doing some drug activity; they searched that Rolls Royce from bumper to bumper, finding nothing. Then I realized that what I had seen in the weeds at that house in the country was actually undercover agents watching our every move.

The police held me there for about forty-five minutes to go over my name and address, the limo company owner's name and address, the name of the place I worked at during the day, and the addresses and phone numbers of everyone there. I couldn't wait to leave. Suddenly I noticed that the police were releasing them. I got back in the Rolls after handing Jeannie the pizza box and her clothes. Don said to the police, "is it all right if I take my pizza now?" They said, "sure."

I couldn't figure out why they were letting them go, so I asked one of the officers. He stated that Don had already been arrested on that warrant; they were just hoping to catch him dealing drugs.

They didn't find any drugs on them or in the car, but I noticed that they never looked under the pizza in the box. It was the only place they didn't look. There isn't much that gets past a chauffeur.

I left the scene and quickly drove back to Ed's house to return the car. His wife greeted me at the door, saying, "Hey, I got a call from the police; do you need a drink?" I said, "Yes! Do you have any Scotch?" She went to the liquor cabinet and grabbed a bottle of Scotch. Then she went to the kitchen cabinet, reached in for a tall water glass, and filled it with ice. She handed both to me while laughing and said, "Tell me about your night." We sat there for about thirty minutes while I told her everything that had happened.

The next day, Ed, being the nerd he was, called me at the law firm, suggesting I split the $145 tip with him. I laughed and almost dropped the phone. I said, "What?" He said I should split the tip with him because it was his company and he had called me to give me that job. He made it sound as though he had done me a favor by calling me and asking me to drive. Actually, he'd had no choice; the other driver hadn't been available. I told him he was crazy to think he was entitled to even half of my tips after what I went through. I was the one that did the driving, I was the one that had to put up with the smart-ass drug dealer, and I was the one that was almost blown away by under cover cops.

The next day at the law firm, I had to answer more questions from the police and the head attorney, as well as from the others I worked with. Everyone was so intrigued by the story that nobody was getting any work done. It was so bad that the head attorney asked if I would like to go home for the day and get some rest. I said, "sure."

It was six months later when I saw an article in the newspaper about Don. It had his name, and it gave the specifics of the charges against him; he received twenty years without parole.

I kept the tip of $145, but I aged ten years that night.

So much for trick-or-treating; I never liked dressing up for Halloween.

IRENE AND BERNIE GET MARRIED

After driving for many weddings—too many to count—I was asked to drive for a Jewish wedding. I hadn't driven for a Jewish wedding and had never been to temple. This wedding was going to be an eye opener, and I was a bit excited at the prospect.

The driving job would be split into two parts: the first would be to pick up the bride and groom after the ceremony at temple, and drive around for fifteen or twenty minutes, and then take them back for pictures and the reception, and the second part of the job would be to pick them up after the reception and take them to a downtown hotel.

I arrived ahead of schedule as usual, and I parked the limo right in front of the doors of the temple. I began to prepare the car by placing the

"Just Married" sign on the rear bumper, setting up the champagne bucket in the stand, and having glasses and napkins ready. The sign for the rear bumper was a bit embarrassing; it was the handmade reversible sign with "Happy Birthday" on the other side.

I was all prepared and standing by the limo with my tuxedo looking as sharp as a chauffeur could when I noticed one of the bridesmaids walking toward me and carrying a gift. She introduced herself, and as she handed the gift to me, she explained what I was to do with it. The gift was to be held by me on the floor in the front seat and was to be kept upright; I was not to let it tip over. She said she would let the bride and groom know. She also mentioned that they would tell me when they wanted to open it.

I thought about this and tried to imagine the contents. The box was about fifteen inches tall and six inches by six inches square. *What could be inside that couldn't tip over?* I thought. It obviously contained liquid, but I was serving champagne, so I thought to myself that liquor was out. I was often put in the position of accepting gifts at weddings and being told what to do with them. Most of the time, the gifts contained money that the giver wanted only the bride and groom to see. So I complied and put the present on the front floor and resumed my position of standing with the back door of the Rolls open, the champagne bottle iced, and glasses ready for the bride and groom. Shortly after this, I noticed several people filing out of the temple and standing prepared to toss birdseed at the bride and groom as they made their way to the limo.

The temple doors swung open, and out came the bride and groom. Both were smiling and as they walked toward the limo; they were being pelted in the usual manner with birdseed and everyone yelling "Congratulations!" This always made me smile, and as they approached the limo, I popped the cork on the champagne bottle, and it started to overflow. I filled their glasses. It was a perfect scene. At that point in weddings, everyone always applauds and cheers as they click pictures. As the bride and groom stood by the limo, I topped off their glasses with champagne again, preparing for them to toast. The bride and groom raised their glasses to the crowd, said thank you, turned toward each other, and interlocked their arms holding the glasses and sipped the champagne. After a quick sip of champagne, they kissed, which of course started the cameras clicking again and brought another cheer from the crowd. Everyone loved the scene; it made for beautiful pictures and lots of memories.

They thanked everyone again and turned to me, saying, “let’s go.” I helped the bride get into the back seat with her massive, gorgeous gown as the groom circled the car to get in the back seat from the other side. I placed the champagne bucket on the floor by the groom and put the stand in the trunk of the car. Just about everyone with a camera wanted to get a snapshot of the bride and groom in the back seat of the Rolls, which took a few minutes.

I closed the doors and proceeded to get behind the wheel. As I started the car, I introduced myself to them. Their names were Irene and Bernie. They thanked me and commented on how beautiful the car was and how much everyone enjoyed taking pictures of it. I started the car and began to drive away from the temple as the guests took pictures of the classic Rolls gracefully pulling away.

We had barely exited the parking lot of the temple when Bernie asked, “did anyone give you a gift for us?” “Yes,” I said. “I have it right here.” I reached over and grabbed the gift I had placed on the floor and handed it over the back seat to them. They were like kids in a candy store, opening the box frantically. We were about to get onto the freeway when the groom asked if I could try to lose the three cars that were following us. I said, "of course; hold on."

I punched the gas pedal, and within about ten seconds the speedometer read 90. There were no cars able to follow us, and we were cruising down the highway. That Rolls Royce was a classic, and it had a very smooth ride, especially at high speed, as it was built to move. I noticed that the bride was whispering something to the groom, and I thought to myself that these two were going to have sex; I just knew it. It amazed me what people would do in a limo! The groom spoke up and asked, "is it okay if we party in here?" I said, "feel free; the car is yours." That pretty little gift box had everything a drug addict would want. I could see in the rearview mirror everything she was pulling out of it. First was a bong filled with water! Next came a little bag of pot followed by a vile of cocaine, a mirror, a razor blade, and a short little straw for snorting. I just laughed. I kept driving as the two of them indulged themselves into a purple haze. They seemed to be having the best of times while listening to the music, snorting, and puffing. The only thing I asked of them was to not burn the leather seats. They responded at the same time by saying, "oh no, we wouldn't do that."

We drove around for about twenty minutes and then headed back to the temple for pictures and the reception. As we pulled up to the temple, Irene asked if I would be the driver picking them up to take them to their hotel later that evening. I said I would be there and gave them the specific time to look for me out front. They responded by saying, "Great." Then they asked if I could secure their little stash of drugs until later. I told them that I had a secret compartment in the boot of the Rolls and that it would be waiting for them.

Several hours passed, and it soon was time to head to the temple reception hall to pick them up and take them to their hotel in downtown. As I approached the temple, I noticed that the woman who had given their present to me was standing out front. I pulled up to the door and stopped the car as she walked toward me. As I got out of the car, she had a big smile on her face, and she thanked me for taking care of Irene and Bernie. I told her it was my pleasure; they really seemed to enjoy the car.

We laughed, as we both knew exactly how much they enjoyed the ride. She then extended her hand out to shake mine, and as we were shaking hands, I felt her handing something off to me being as discretely as possible. It was a fifty-dollar bill wrapped around a little gift for me—cocaine! I thanked her and put it in my pocket. She replied by saying, "I'll see you later, okay?" I responded by saying, "okay," not knowing what she was talking about, but assuming that she meant at the hotel that evening. No one had mentioned it to me, but it sounded as though I was going to be invited back to the hotel with the bride and groom to party with their friends. This sort of invitation came often as a limo driver; more than anyone can imagine. It must be the tuxedo.

Soon after she went back into the reception hall, the groom came out to the car. He informed me that there was going to be a party at the hotel that would be going late into the evening, and he invited me to join them. The entire bridal party consisted of friends from the college he and Irene attended in Florida. Bernie said that Irene insisted that I join them. I mentioned that it sounded like fun and thanked him for the invite. I also said that I would take them to the hotel and drop the rolls off at the garage before joining them. I thanked him, and we stood there talking about the Rolls for a few minutes before he went back into the reception hall. The night was young, and I thought about going to the party with enthusiasm. They seemed like a very nice couple, and I had a feeling it would be a fun party.

Moments later, the reception hall doors opened, and there they were, the bride and groom, heading for the Rolls. I got out of the front seat and opened the back doors for them to get in. They were having a great time, but as is the case with most couples on their wedding days, they had had enough of relatives and wanted to change clothes and relax with friends.

It only took about ten minutes to get to the hotel. It was one of the more expensive hotels downtown, and on the way they explained that Bernie's father had rented an entire floor of the hotel for all of the bridal party. I was amazed, and I thought about how expensive that must have been an mentioned something about it. Irene spoke up and said, "Yes, our parents have shelled out a ton of money for this wedding, to the tune of over fifty thousand dollars." All I could say was "Wow." As we pulled up to the front of the hotel, the bellhop came to the car and opened their door. I handed the box that contained the party goods to the groom. Bernie looked at it as I mentioned to him that I had wrapped it back up. He thanked me and asked again if I would be coming back. I told him I would be back in about twenty minutes. He said, "Great, the others would like to meet you." By this he meant the entire bridal party and their other friends.

I proceeded back to the garage to clean the car. As I was cleaning the car, I noticed that the groom had left his hat in the back seat, so I put it in my car to take back to him. It was about a half hour later when I arrived at the hotel. They had given me the room number, so I found my way to their floor and located the room. It wasn't hard to find the room; all I had to do was follow the noise from the party. I knocked on the door and soon heard a voice asking, "Who is it?" I replied by saying, "Ric, the chauffeur." The door opened quickly, and a hand grabbed my arm and pulled me into the room rather swiftly. There was good reason, as the room was full of smoke, and it wasn't cigarette smoke. I soon had a glass of champagne in my hand, and people were passing joint after joint. The bedroom was where the cocaine was; there was an unimaginable amount. These kids were party animals. I partied with them for about ninety minutes, talking to everyone and having a great time. When I decided to leave, the bride and groom walked over and thanked me, both kissing me on opposite sides of my face and telling me that I had done a great job that day and that the pictures were going to be great. He handed me an envelope, and inside was a hundred-dollar tip. He jokingly said that he had almost forgotten it. I laughed and thought to myself, *no wonder, with all of the drugs they were doing*. The envelope also had a piece of paper with their Florida address and phone number. He said to look them up if I was ever in Florida.

I never did contact them, but as with all of the unusual weddings that I've driven for I do think of them often and just laugh. This was the only Jewish wedding I ever drove for, and I would not soon forget it.

ONE DAY, THREE WEDDINGS

This particular Saturday was like most—filled with weddings. The only difference was that it was winter. I had driven for several weddings in one day during the summer, but not in the winter. You never know what the weather is going to be like, and icy roads could spell disaster in the Rolls Royce. It was the weekend before Christmas and apparently a popular day for weddings. I was scheduled to drive for three that day. Normally, there wasn't a problem with back-to-back weddings during the summer because of dry roads and the ability to drive fast without the worry of snow and ice. Winter weddings afforded one luxury though—not sweating in the black tuxedo. It was a nice change of pace. All three weddings were in different parts of town, which seemed to be the way it always was. Just as I would finish one wedding, I would have to race across town to get to the next one. Most of the time picture-taking sessions would run over and cause me to run late for the next wedding. Almost every wedding I had driven for had run over the time reserved because of the pictures. There were several weddings that I had worked at for which planners had not taken into account how long the pictures would take with consideration for the limousine. For example, if a wedding ceremony was scheduled to start at 1:00 p.m. and last for an hour, ending around 2:00 p.m., they would rent the limousine for an hour and request it to be there from 2:00 p.m. to 3:00 p.m. But the pictures would more than likely take at least an hour. If I had weddings that were back-to-back and the bride and groom didn't come out to the car by the end of their booked hour, I would have to leave to make it to the next wedding on time. This just added a little stress to my day, and you can imagine how unhappy the bride and groom would be as they came out of the church, expecting to see a limousine and finding that I was gone. This also equated to no tip for me, which didn't make me very happy.

I was being paid five dollars an hour by Ed, and I had inquired about a raise on many occasions, but he never would even consider it. One thing I have learned in business is the fact that if an employer doesn't take good care of the employees (who, by the way, are on the frontline where they are dealing directly with their customers) an atmosphere of mutiny festers. Unhappy employees usually have the key to sabotage or destroy a business, often without being detected until it is too late for the owner. In this case, I was driving and responsible for a classic old Rolls Royce valued in the range of over one hundred thousand dollars by today's standards, and I could have easily been distracted while driving, which could cause and accident. This meant that if an accident occurred, having only one car would halt the business until repairs had been made. But Ed didn't seem to care about that.

I arrived early for the first wedding of the day, and as I sat in front of the church while watching the guests exit, I realized that this one might run over. There was about fifteen minutes left on the hour they had booked, and I started to worry as I realized that I needed at least twenty minutes to drive them to the reception hall. Time was running out, and there was nothing I could do, so I went into the church to see how the picture-taking session was going. Well, it wasn't going as planned. I clearly could see that there were many pictures yet to be taken. I looked at my watch and saw that there was now only ten minutes left on their hour.

If I didn't have another wedding to go to, I would normally wait in this situation, letting them run over their time and leaving it up to Ed to collect for the additional time. But on this day I needed to leave at a designated time.

I knew this wedding party was not going to be pleased, and I didn't want to hang around to catch the flack. Additionally, I didn't want to have two wedding parties upset with me; one was enough in one day.

Realizing that the pictures were taking the full hour and knowing that I could not wait any longer, I started to pack everything back into the Rolls Royce trunk. Just as I had everything packed into the trunk, I noticed one of the groomsmen coming out of the front door of the church and walking toward the Rolls. I looked at him and asked if he was the person that had booked the car. He replied with a proud yes. I introduced myself and broke the bad news to him, mentioning that I unfortunately could not wait any longer, as I had another wedding to do. This guy understandably became very upset with me and began asking how I could just leave. I told him that the hour he had rented the car for had just ended and that because there was another wedding on the schedule, I had to leave. He quickly said, "how about my money?" He wanted a refund, and he seemed to expect that I could give it to him at that moment. I informed him that I did not carry cash with me, which seemed to light a fuse and set him on fire. I said, "Sir, I see here that you gave a credit card." He said, "Yes, I did." I replied by saying, "well, you will need to work that out with the owner of the limo service." I then added, "I was here at the designated time and was here for the full hour that you requested and paid for. I really don't think that we'll be able to refund your money." He went off on me, calling me every name in the book. The man had just come out of church, and he had no problem taking the Lord's name in vain. I knew I had to get out of that situation without damage to the Rolls Royce, so I quickly mentioned again that he needed to call the owner and work it out with him. Then the guy said, "well, then how in the hell will the bride and groom get to the reception?" I replied by saying, "unfortunately, I can't do anything about that, sir; I need to leave." When I closed my door, I noticed he was walking toward the car with a threatening posture. He was acting as though he was going to do some damage to make up for the money he had lost.

So I reached my hand under the front seat to grab my trusty friend, Mr. Tire Iron. I opened the door and got out of the Rolls Royce and walked toward him, holding the tire iron in hand, and I said, "get away from the car and go back into the church. This is not my first day at the rodeo." He suddenly realized that I was not kidding, and it seemed he was pretty sure he would have a tire iron for a hat if he touched the car. My heart was pounding, and I was thinking I was about to get into a fight when he had a change of heart. He looked at the tire iron in my hand, looked at me, and without saying another word, he turned around and went back into the church. I was shaking inside, and I suddenly realized that he was going back into the church to get help. Well, I got back in that Rolls Royce faster than you could blink. I started the engine, threw it in drive and hit the gas. The tires were spitting stones all over the place as I sped out of the parking lot. Once I got onto the main road I began to calm down, but at the same time, I looked at my watch and realized I was going to be cutting it close in getting to the second wedding.

On several occasions while I was standing in front of churches or restaurants while waiting for clients, individuals would approach the car, most of them intoxicated or under the influence of some type of drug, wanting to get in the car or acting like the car had arrived for them. You know, showing off for those around them. I had had enough of that attitude by this point in my driving career, and I could quickly spot those types of troublemakers. Thus, Mr. Tire Iron always rode first class, under the front seat, offering me needed security at times.

The situations of back-to-back weddings could have been avoided if only Ed would have tried to give at least an hour between bookings. Most people don't realize how much time pictures take after a ceremony. Heck, it takes at least thirty minutes to organize the bridal party, and then it takes time to shift everyone around for the next picture. But Ed only saw the dollar signs, and he didn't want to say no to anyone calling for the car unless he absolutely had to. Consideration for schedules wasn't at the top of his list, because he didn't have to deal with the angry customers face-to-face.

My thought on why he gave me crazy bookings goes back to the night my customers were busted by the vice squad and Ed asked me for half the tip. To this day it makes my blood boil when I think of him asking me to split that tip with him. The nerve! I began to notice a pattern with the wedding bookings that he would give to me. Basically, if someone was renting the limousine for a bride and groom, Ed would ask them what their relationship was to the bride and groom. If they were not in the bridal party, nor were they a relative, nine times out of ten they would not be around during the job, meaning there would be no tip for the driver. I couldn't expect the bride and groom to tip; after all, the car was a gift to them. Many of the weddings that I did went on without me getting a tip; plenty of smiles, but no tip. Ed seemed to get a kick out it, and he suggested I arrive early to hunt down the person who had rented the limo and introduce myself. Well, that would work if time would have allowed it, but it seemed I had no breathing room between jobs. I pretty much only received back-to-back driving jobs, which make for stressful days. I arrived at the second wedding just in time to set up the champagne and be standing alongside the Rolls Royce before the guests started to exit the church after the ceremony. The person who had rented the limo for the bride and groom introduced himself and even had an envelope with a tip enclosed. Of course this made me smile as I thought of the situation I had just come from. I thought my holiday spirit was lost, but my confidence was quickly renewed. Everything was going as planned; the bride and groom exited the church and approached the car while everyone was tossing birdseed and saying congratulations. Cameras were clicking, and everyone appeared to be having a great time—except for the bride and groom.

As I was filling their champagne glasses, I sensed a bit of tension between the two of them. They were smiling for the crowd, but they didn't act as though they had just been married and were on their way to a new and joyful life together; something was up.

It appeared almost humorous as the bride was glaring at the groom at times and was avoiding his advances. It was clear she was very upset, and all I could think of was that the three of us were about to get into the Rolls Royce.

The bride and groom finished toasting each other and indicated that they were ready to head to the reception. I helped the bride into the back seat, stuffing the dress in where I could without wrinkling it too much. Basically, her gown was two sizes too big for that back seat, but we managed to get her in with the dress on.

I got a kick out of some of the wedding dresses I saw while driving the limo. Some were just massive and looked great while the bride was standing; however, trying to cram them into a back seat was a different story. This bride had a hoop skirt, and we all know what happens to a hoop skirt if you don't sit on it properly. You guessed it, that hoop just flew up in her face. We tried to fix it, but we realized the only way she could ride comfortably was to pull the dress up with the hoop part behind her. This was comical to say the least! She had to hike her dress up to her waist, exposing the underworld, and it was cold out. Believe me, I saw everything! So I quickly put myself between her and guests that were watching to shield her from the embarrassment of exposing herself. She wasn't in the best of moods prior to this, and you can bet this didn't help matters at all. She grew increasingly agitated by the second. We finally got everything in the back seat, and I closed the doors for them and got in the front seat to start the car and head to the reception. As we were pulling away from the church, cameras were clicking and the guests were tossing birdseed at the car as usual. I looked into the rearview mirror and noticed that the bride and groom were not even sitting remotely close to each other. Up to this point, not one word had been spoken in the back seat. So I thought that I should break the ice, and I asked the question that seemed to start world war three. I said, "So, how is everything going so far?"

Without a reply to me, the bride blurted out in the angriest tone to the groom, "I have had enough of your mother. If she makes one more comment about anything she thinks isn't the way she would have done it, I promise I will knock her on her ass in front of everyone!" The groom replied by saying, "Okay honey, I'm sorry, but I can't control her." The bride added, "When we get to the reception, *keep her away from me*. You need to let her know that this is my day and this is how I want everything to go, and tell her to keep her mouth shut." He replied by saying, "Okay, I'll talk to her." Then the bride said, "Is this the way our marriage is going to be, her butting in to our lives?" The groom said, "honey, relax, don't let her get to you." The bride reiterated her previous statement, saying, "I'm serious; I'll knock her on her ass in front of everyone. I'm tired of her mouth!"

Well now, that was not the response I had expected, but I did get the two of them talking again. After that kind of a start to their marriage, who knows what the future holds. As you can imagine, I didn't say another word until we arrived at the reception hall and I stopped the car and opened the doors for them to get out. I congratulated them both as we shook hands, and then I wished them the best of luck.

The groom turned to me as they were walking away from the car; he rolled his eyes and lipped, "Help me." I just shook my head to say no and smiled back and said, "fasten your seat belt." They thanked me, and I closed the doors and proceeded to get into the car to head to the third wedding of the day. So far this had been the most eventful wedding day in my driving career, and little did I know that it was about to get better; I just had no idea. As I headed to do my third wedding of the day, I began to reflect on how the day had gone so far and how unbelievable it had been. I knew exactly where the next church was, and I had plenty of time to get there, mostly because the bride and groom at the previous wedding had just wanted to get the day over with. They didn't much feel like joy riding in the limo.

The next church I was heading to was a huge Catholic church on the north side of town. When I arrived, I noticed that the parking lot was packed with what appeared to be more than a hundred cars. This was going to be a big wedding. The best man had paid for this job and had included a fifty-dollar tip for the driver. As I pulled up to the church, a very sharply dressed man walked toward the car. He introduced himself; he was the best man. I quickly thanked him for the tip, and he replied by saying, "Thank you . . . and take them wherever they want to go before dropping them off at the reception hall." I said, "Absolutely!" He shook my hand and winked as he turned to head back into the church. I opened the trunk to start my preparation of the champagne presentation. Just as I was getting glasses and napkins out of the trunk, I heard someone yelling, "That's for me!" I looked toward the front of the church, and the groom was standing there with a huge smile on his face. He grabbed his brother, the best man, and was thanking him as they walked toward me. The best man introduced his brother as they were looking the car over. All he could say was, "Wow! Thank you, brother!" The three of us chatted for a few minutes, and then they looked at each other, saying that they should probably go back into the church, as the ceremony was about to start. I said, "Good luck, I'll see you later." The groom replied by saying, "I can't wait." I stood by the Rolls Royce as the last of the guests were filing into the church. That always makes for a nice presentation, and Ed always wants free advertising. After about fifteen minutes, I could hear the music playing, and I assumed that the bride was walking down the aisle. I kept standing by the car. I had lit a cigarette and was puffing away and waiting for my cue to do my part when I suddenly could hear what sounded like people screaming. I looked around and realized that it was coming from the church.

Almost immediately afterward, the guests started filing out of the church. I thought to myself that this didn't seem right; the guests were leaving! They also were not standing around in front of the church like normal wedding guests do. Most usually hang out to toss birdseed at the bride and groom as they run to the limo. These people were walking straight to their cars. I stood there just looking at them, and finally a couple walked by me, saying, "I wouldn't count on driving the bride and groom today. It appears there is not going to be a wedding." I said, "what?" Then they explained that they couldn't hear well because they had been in the back of the church, but they told me that the bride had been talking to the congregation when a fistfight had suddenly broken out at the front of the church. The father of the bride had gone after the groom. Everyone had started after them to break it up. People had started screaming. Then they had decided to leave, so they didn't know exactly what happened, but they did know the wedding was off. I couldn't believe what I was hearing, and I just stood there in shock and disbelief. I waited in front of the church, and after about fifteen minutes, the best man appeared at the doorway of the church. He looked at me and headed directly toward the car. I could tell that he had a bruise on his face that hadn't been there before, so I said, "what is going on?" He replied by saying, "You're not going to believe this." He proceeded to tell me that they had had a bachelor party on Friday night before the wedding and that the maid of honor had showed up. I looked at him, shocked. He then continued, saying, "You guessed it, my brother poked her, and his fiancée found out about it." Well, you could have knocked me over with a feather. I couldn't believe what I was hearing. Then he said, "A huge fight broke out, and the bride's father went after the groom. It was a big mess, and the wedding is off." I replied by saying, "I guess so." Then I told him to call Ed the next day and explain the situation so that he might be able to get a refund. I asked him if he wanted a bottle of champagne and he replied by saying, "Yes, let's open it and have a drink." I said, "Okay, but let me pull the car around the back of the church." He said, "I'll meet you around back." So I put the champagne in the back seat and proceeded to pull the car around back. There stood the best man with two other groomsmen when I approached. I noticed they were all laughing, and as I got out of the car, I realized and thought to myself, *What else is there to do at this point but laugh.* I served the boys the champagne until it was gone. We stood there as they re-enacted the scene, and after about thirty minutes, I told them I needed to leave. One of the guys said to me, "I bet this has never happened before." I replied by saying, "You're right." I couldn't believe how this day had turned out—three very awkward situations. It started on a bad note and ended the same. It truly was an eventful day that I will never forget!

THE BACHELORETTE PARTY

I must admit that by this time in my driving career, I had had my limit of babysitting intoxicated adults. There's nothing wrong with having a few drinks, but enough is enough, and I had already contemplated my so-called retirement as a professional chauffeur, having hit the burnout stage. After driving for almost six years, one of my biggest disappointments was the lack of a raise. That, in addition to my receiving the less desirable driving jobs, just kept pressing on my mind, and I became more irritated. Being a chauffeur can be a lot of fun and is exciting at times, but I couldn't pick and choose my clients, and as they say, a few can ruin it for the larger group.

This day would involve two jobs, with the first being a wedding in the afternoon. I would be driving a convertible Rolls Royce that Ed rented from a private owner on an as-needed basis; it was a 1980 Rolls Royce Corniche convertible.

The second job would take place four hours later and would involve driving for a bachelorette party for a total of five hours. The car I would use for that was a 1983 Lincoln stretch limousine. Ed had purchased it toward the end of my driving career, and he had hired other drivers as well. The Lincoln was a dark navy blue with a dark blue leather interior. It had the usual limousine features: a glass divider between the driver and the passengers, a color television, a liquor cabinet, and very dark windows.

There were also telephones for the driver and the passengers so they could communicate without lowering the glass divider. The passengers could see through the glass divider; however, the chauffeur could not, as the glass was a one-way mirror.

I began my day with the Rolls Royce Corniche convertible, which was a light yellow cream color on the outside with a white leather interior. It was beautiful, and with the convertible top down, it was a blast to drive. Occasionally, if I had a long break between jobs, I would visit friends and give them a ride in the Rolls. Most of the time, they would request to go through a drive through at a fast food restaurant. That was always fun for them. On this particular job, I needed to pick up the Corniche early that morning, since the owner lived on the far east side of town and the driving job was on the far north side of town.

My cousin Lori was getting married on this afternoon, but I had two driving jobs that day and could only attend the latter part of her reception. My partner was going to attend Lori's wedding, so I told him I would take him in the Rolls, do my driving job, and then come to the reception and pick him up. We would then take the Corniche back to the owner since I would be using the stretch Lincoln for the bachelorette party that evening.

It was an extremely hot August afternoon; the temperature was ninety-six degrees and the sky was clear, so we decided to put the convertible top down to enjoy the sunshine. That car was fun to drive and was very impressive. We were about ten minutes away from Lori's reception when we were stopped at a traffic light. It seemed like the traffic light had a very long cycle. There was a lot of traffic backed up at the light, and we were now sitting through the second red light. With the hot sun beating down on us, it appeared as though we were baking. I turned to him and said, "I could put the top and the windows up and turn on the air conditioning if you want." He quickly responded with a yes. I mean, it was a cooker that day. In order to put the convertible top up, the transmission needed to be in park. So, knowing that I had plenty of time before the light turned green, I moved the gear selector to Park. Next I started to put the windows up by pushing the buttons. Well, nothing happened. The windows didn't move. I looked at him and said, "something is wrong; the windows are not working." He just looked at me in disbelief. I next tried the button that brought the convertible top up, but nothing happened. By this time the light had turned green, so I decided to try the windows and top later. I moved the gear lever into drive and nothing happened. Then the engine died. I looked at him, and all I could say was, "I don't need this right now." He replied by saying, "what are we going to do?" There we were, stuck in traffic with a dead Rolls Royce. People were driving by us, and some were laughing. You can only imagine how we felt. We had to push the Rolls off to the side of the road. That was a funny sight, as both of us were dressed up. This being the time period before everyone had a cell phone, I needed to walk to a pay phone. I started walking when a couple in a Jeep Cherokee slowed down beside me and asked if they could give me a ride anywhere. I said, "yes, I would appreciate that." Doug was sitting with the car; we couldn't leave it alone, as the top and windows were down. The couple in the Jeep took me to a hotel, which was about a quarter of a mile away from where the car broke down. I tried calling Ed and there was no answer. The other phone number I had was that of the owner of the Corniche. I really hesitated in calling him but I had to reach someone that could help with towing that car. The owner would know exactly what to do, whom to call, and where to take the car. I reluctantly dialed his number, and after the phone rang four or five times, someone picked up the phone. It was the owner of the Corniche. I explained who I was and told him that the car had broken down. He quickly said, "what happened, did the electrical system go out again?" I responded, "it must have." Then I told him what was happening, and he knew immediately what the problem was. He began cursing the electrical system that Rolls Royce used in that model. Apparently this was a common problem, but I wish I had known there was this issue. I never would have taken this car out if I had known there was the possibility of a breakdown. Now, I still had the issue of the wedding I was supposed to drive for. I called the church where the wedding was being held and asked the church secretary to pass along to the bride and groom that the limousine had broken down. She said, "I'm so sorry. I know they were looking forward to it." I asked her to apologize for me, but there was nothing I could do. I hung up the phone and headed back to the car and Doug. It took about fifteen minutes to walk back to the car, where he was sitting in the baking heat with no shade. When I approached, he was laughing. He mentioned that just about everyone who had gone by had made a comment about the flashy, broken-down car. How embarrassing! I told him that I had reached the owner by phone and that he was calling a tow truck to take the car to a garage. Apparently this was an issue that the mechanic had not worked out yet. Doug decided to walk to the reception, and I told him that I would just meet him at home later that evening after the bachelorette job. He said, "goodbye and good luck," as he started walking.

Later that evening he told me that it had taken him ninety minutes to get to Lori's reception and that he had been soaked from sweating in the blazing heat. I guess the restaurant was a bit farther than we had thought. We had a good laugh about it after the fact, but he has never let me forget it.

Well, the tow truck came and picked up the Corniche as planned. The driver asked if he could drop me off someplace. I said, "yes, that would be great." So, with the Rolls Royce on the back of the flatbed tow truck, I proceeded to give him directions to my home, which was about twenty minutes away. When we arrived at my house, I thanked him for the ride and got out of the truck. I couldn't believe what had happened, but my day was not over. I badly needed to take a shower; I had been sweating from the heat too. After relaxing in the cool air conditioning of my house, I started to get dressed for the bachelorette party. By that time the sun was going down, and it was starting to cool off outside to a cool eighty degrees. I headed to the garage to get the stretch Lincoln and went into the garage where Ed had a refrigerator packed with bottles of champagne. This job called for two bottles of champagne and eight glasses. I quickly knew that I was going to be driving eight women. The specifics of this job were that I was to pick up seven of the women at their homes and take them to the house where the bachelorette party was. They also had a list of bars they wanted to go to after spending a couple of hours at the party.

All of the bars were in the campus area on High Street. This was *the* hangout for all of the college students, and I knew there was going to be a lot of traffic both on foot and in cars. I proceeded to read the requested order in which they wanted to be picked up. After acclimating myself with the maps and the location of each house, I headed off to start my journey. Each pickup went off like clockwork. The women enjoyed being treated like royalty as I got out and opened the door for them. By the time I picked up the seventh, they were chattering, and they all seemed to be talking at the same time in the back of the limo. They had the stereo on while watching TV. I thought to myself, *how can they hear each other; they're all talking at the same time.* I really got a kick out of it. We soon approached the house where the party was. It was a new house in a new development. There was a long road leading to a cul-de-sac with open fields all around it. I pulled up to the front of the house and opened the doors; out came seven women ready to party. They each had gifts for the bride-to-be, and I helped carry them into the house. Several women were already inside, and they were drinking and laughing and having a good time. I soon realized that I was the only man there. I felt a bit out of place, but I had nowhere to go. The bride-to-be had paid for the limo for five hours, meaning I needed to stay there and couldn't drive around and come back at a designated time. I neatly placed the gifts on the gift table and went back out to the

Lincoln to straighten up the trunk and back seat. As I was straightening up the car, the bride-to-be came out and started talking to me about the car. She asked if I liked being a limo driver and what it was like to drive a stretch limousine. I entertained her with my answers, making her laugh at some of the situations I had been in. She said, "Well, you know you don't have to stay outside. You can come in and watch TV upstairs if you want." I said, "That would be nice." She then said, "don't worry; I won't let any of the women bother you." I just laughed and thanked her. We walked back into the house, and as I walked by the living room, I noticed that a movie projector had been set up on the coffee table. Now, there's only one reason for a movie projector to be at a bachelorette party, and that's to show dirty movies. I thought, *great, I'm going to be upstairs in a bedroom with twenty women watching porn downstairs in the living room and getting hornier by the minute.* This didn't seem to be a situation I really wanted to be in. I went up to the bedroom and turned on the TV. The bride-to-be also brought snacks and a beer for me, so I was all set. After a few minutes, I could hear that they were all playing some sort of game. I'd never been to a bridal shower or bachelorette party, so I had no clue what they were doing. I just know they were having a lot of fun and laughing hysterically at times. I had been watching TV for about forty-five minutes when I heard a knock on the bedroom door. It opened, and there was the bride-to-be with somewhat of an embarrassed look on her face. I said hello, and she walked toward me. I could tell she had a question. She said, "Ric, Do you know anything about projectors?" I just cracked up laughing and said yes. She asked if I could come downstairs and fix their projector; they couldn't get it to work. I agreed to fix the projector, and we headed downstairs toward the living room. As I appeared at the bottom of the stairs, the women broke out in applause and a chant. They were all clapping, and they were chanting "stripper, stripper, stripper." I just laughed and walked over to the projector while saying "no, no, no; Ric doesn't strip." They got a big kick out it, and I was thankfully able to quickly thread the film through the projector and get it operating. When I turned it on, it was right in the middle of a hot and heavy sex scene. Now, normally I wouldn't be embarrassed at that, but I was in the middle of a pack of wolves that made it clear exactly what they wanted—me to undress! I just went back to my television in the bedroom. They had been watching movies for about another thirty minutes when there was a knock on the bedroom door. It was the hostess; she told me that they were ready to go driving around for a bit before the girls were taken home. You couldn't imagine how relieved I was to know we were getting out of there. I quickly headed out the door and made my way to the limousine. As the women came out to the limo, I opened the doors for them to get in the back. I looked up and noticed that one had a bottle of bourbon and another was smoking pot. They began passing the little hand-rolled cigarette around to one another. Well, I thought to myself that this was going to be a rough night. They were ready to party, and I again was the babysitter, and I was not looking forward to it. Luckily, they didn't bring the drugs in the car; they finished them off before they got in. All eight women were in the back of the limo, and they were passing the bottle around, each taking a sip and passing it along. All I could think of was that someone was going to get sick before the night was over, which meant that I would have to clean it up. Passengers in the back seat usually drank, but this was out of hand before we started off to the bars. The first thing that people do when they get into the back of the limo is play with all of the buttons and switches. This was the case, and the glass divider went up and down several times. They picked up the phone and buzzed me at least ten times, asking for James. That was the favorite name that people had for the driver, and it was getting old. They opened and closed the sunroof several times. It really was annoying, and I didn't like the way they were flaunting the bottle of booze. They had the windows down, and as we would pass cars, they would hold up the bottle as to toast the other drivers. Well, this was not good, and I didn't feel like explaining anything to the police in the event we were pulled over. They could have gotten away with it, but I had had two beers. Having the master controls up front by the driver was the best part about this limousine. I turned down the stereo and lowered the glass divider. Looking at the back seat, I said, "please do not flaunt the bottle of booze out the window, we could get pulled over, and none of us want that, okay?" They all replied in a snotty tone by saying, "okay, sorry." Then someone in the back seat pushed the button for the glass divider to go back up. As I mentioned earlier, the glass divider was one-way glass, and I couldn't see through it unless I looked through the rearview mirror. Then I could see into the back seat perfectly. Well, as you can imagine, I received a couple middle fingers for asking them not to hold the bottle of booze out the window. I didn't let on, but I was saving that for later. Maybe I would say something at the end of the evening after I received a tip—but not until then.

We approached the campus area, and as I expected, traffic was bad and there were mobs of people walking on both sides of the street while moving from bar to bar. I just knew that the windows were going to go down and that the bottle of booze was going to be shown to everyone. It wasn't five minutes later when I heard one of the girls in the back seat yelling at people on the sidewalk. She kept repeating "Look at me; I'm Lady Di," as she held up the bottle of booze to the crowd on the sidewalk. I lowered the glass divider, and looking into the back seat, I again said, "please do not hang out the window, showing the bottle of booze to everyone. We could get arrested for having an open container!" Well, this didn't stop her. She kept the window down and kept yelling "Look at me; I'm Lady Di." She kept yelling it over and over and over, to the point that I had had enough. There were police walking the sidewalks, and I wanted no part of that type of an ending to the evening. So, with the master controls at my fingertips, I waited until her arms were inside the window. At the moment I saw her arms were in, I pushed the button and rolled up the window, and then I pushed the master lock control switch. Once the master lock is on, the windows will not go down, nor will the doors unlock. At last! I was in total control with the glass divider up. The next thing I heard was the phone buzzing, so I picked it up. On the other end was the drunken fool that had kept yelling that she was Lady Di. She complained that the windows didn't work. Thinking as quickly as I could, I played along and said, "Let me try the master control switch." Then I said, "They're not working. We must have blown some fuses moving them up and down so much. I won't be able to fix them until I get back to the garage." They all bought it, but as I looked in my rearview mirror, I noticed that her middle finger went up at me again, and she didn't think I could see it. Well, since we were heading to drop everyone off at home and the person that had ordered the limo was not in the limo, it suddenly hit me that I was not going to get a tip for that evening. Here was another crap babysitting job that Ed had given to me. He had also known that the Corniche could possibly have broken down earlier that day, and he didn't want that hassle. So, having had enough of the drunken girls in the back of the limo, I decided to further mess with them. I picked up my phone and hit the buzzer. After a couple of seconds, one of the girls in the back picked up the phone and said, “Hello.” I said, “Does your friend in the red top need a Band-Aid?” She turned to her and said, “The driver wants to know if you need a Band-Aid.” The woman in the red top replied by saying, “No, why?” The girl that had answered the phone repeated that to me. “She said no, why?” I replied by saying, “Well, she keeps holding her middle finger up.” All I could hear was screaming, and then she slammed down the phone. They knew they were busted. I just laughed and proceeded to drive them home. Needless to say, I did not get a tip that evening, but payback for the disrespect was worth more than money could buy.

The following week, I went over to Ed’s to pick up my check. No one was home, so I let myself in and went into the office to look for my check. I found my check, but I also ran across the booking cards for each job I had done the week before. I noticed that two of them had included tips on the charge for the driver—me! I quickly recalculated my hours to see if my check was correct. It was correct, but it did not include those tips. I started thinking about that and realized I had never received any pay on my check except for the exact hours that I worked. I wondered to myself about how many of the jobs during the past six years had paid in advance and included tips that I hadn’t received. I had blamed the clients for being cheap, but I had the wrong person. I did leave Ed a message letting him know that he could include the tip I saw on the charge slip on my next check. I wanted to let him know that I saw it. The next week, I went over to Ed's to go over some upcoming jobs and to pick up my check. Ed was a different person, and he seemed a bit short with me. Of course, I knew why he had an attitude; I had busted him. I had just wanted him to know that I knew what he was doing. As we were going over upcoming jobs, I also mentioned that I would not be available to drive for New Year's Eve that year. I gave him four months notice since this would be my sixth New Year's Eve and I wanted to stay home. He was doing some bookwork at his desk, and he looked up and replied by saying, "Fine, thanks for letting me know well in advance." I wanted to make sure he didn't plan on me driving that New Year's Eve, so every time I talked to his wife, I also mentioned it to her. Well, you guessed it. I had to work at my full-time job until noon on New Year's Eve, and it was about 10:00 a.m. when my phone rang. It was Ed calling to go over the jobs I was going to do that evening. I said, "Ed, what jobs? I told you several times that I was not available." He said, "No you didn't; I have you down as driving tonight." We went back and forth, and he insisted that I did not tell him, but I had also told his wife on several occasions over the previous four months. They knew I had told them. They wanted to let one of the other drivers off for the evening, and he thought he could bully me into driving. Then he said, "So you mean I can't run my business?" I said, "It means that you and your wife have hearing problems." I went on to tell him that I was having guests over for dinner, so there was no way I would be driving the limo. Ed would not get off of the phone, and he kept insisting that I would be driving that evening. Well, he didn't win that one. I hung up on him, and that was the last time I ever talked to him. As far as I was concerned, I had reached the end of my rope.

THE GOLDEN OPPORTUNITY!

It was about two years after I had driven professionally that I was asked to drive again. This time it would not be for a limousine service. I had had my fill of that type of client and was burned out with that line of work. I had always had a full-time day job during the week, and I was a bartender in the evenings Monday through Thursday. This left Friday evening through Sunday open for driving jobs with the limousine company. Yes, at times I was working three jobs and loving the money, but that also takes its toll on a person and relationships. On various occasions while driving as a professional chauffeur, clients would ask for good restaurant suggestions. I would ask what type of food they had in mind. When they would say Italian, I would always suggest my cousin Stella's restaurant. It was called Casa di Pasta, which in Italian means "house of pasta." Casa di Pasta was located in the north campus area and was decorated in a traditional Italian style. There was a lot of red-flocked floral wallpaper and statues reminiscent of Italy. My mother had helped Stella fine tune the various recipes in addition to teaching other waitresses to greet guests in Italian. It was always a lot of fun to go to the restaurant, as Stella was a character that was larger than life. She was always happy to see us. Stella had had four children: two girls and two boys. The youngest boy had been two months younger than I was, and his name was also Ricky. We were always referred to as Ricky One and Ricky Two. While living about a half mile apart in a close-knit Italian community called San Margarita, we frequently played together and often got into trouble, as children do. When we were twelve years old, tragedy struck. Ricky was riding his bike on his way home when he was hit and killed by a car. To me, this was the worst of tragedies. At the time, I felt that had I lost my best friend. We had frequently been together, as our mothers would often babysit for each other's kids. I will never forget that funeral, and the vision of seeing him—my best friend and second cousin—in the casket is as clear in my mind now as it was the day it happened. From that point on, Stella would always tear up when she would see me, calling me Ricky One and kissing and hugging me tightly, as I reminded her of her son. It always made me feel good, but at the same time I knew that I triggered those tragic memories in her mind. Ricky Two is always in my mind.

One Saturday afternoon, while we were sitting in the back yard, the phone rang. I saw Stella's name on the caller ID, so I picked up the phone. She greeted me in the usual Italian tone that she used. Her character was larger than life. After we chatted a while, she asked if I was still driving the limo. I told her that I hadn't driven the limo for quite a while, and she asked if I thought I would want to do it again. I told her I would, but not for a limousine company. She proceeded to tell me about a girlfriend of hers that had come into the restaurant the night before. Her girlfriend was married to a doctor, and they lived in the north end of town, but they were looking to move closer to the hospital he was currently working at. Stella went on to tell me that he had just purchased a twenty-two-foot Cadillac stretch limousine and was looking for someone to drive for them on a part-time basis, and she asked if I would be interested in meeting them. I told her I absolutely would! She mentioned that the doctor and his wife had driven the limo to the restaurant, but they needed someone that could handle that big car. Stella said they were looking not only for a driver, but for one that would be able to take care of himself too. That was a curious stipulation, so I asked about it. She went on to say that the doctor had a lot of money and was a Mafioso. Then she added that she thought he was just paranoid in thinking everyone wanted what he had. I didn't think much about it after that and never discussed it again. Then Stella asked if I wanted their phone number to set up a time to meet with them. I replied by saying, "yes! Thank you!"

This marriage was the doctor's third. His wife was thirty-seven years old, and he was fifty-two. Stella told me that the doctor had two sons from his first marriage but that he hadn't spoken to them in years. When I asked why this was, Stella went on to say he had disowned them because the only time they came around was when they wanted money. Well, he did have a lot of money, which helped with his favorite hobby—collecting cars. Stella told me that they lived about thirty-five minutes out of town in a beautiful home that was a temporary move, as they wanted to move closer. I thanked Stella again and told her that I would call them later that evening. After I hung up the phone, I told my partner all about the call and mentioned that the doctor wanted someone that could "take care of himself." We were oddly curious and intrigued as to what type of character this guy was. After talking about it for a while, I decided to call them and at least meet them. The phone rang as I waited for someone to pick up, and then someone did—it was the wife. I introduced myself as Stella's cousin Ric, and she said in an excited tone, "I'm so happy you called; I'm BJ." Then she said, "do you want to drive for us?" I laughed as I thought to myself, *this woman has had too much coffee!* She spoke with a very excited voice that was almost too perky. I replied by saying, "yes!" That was all I had to say. She talked as though she had known me for years, chatting about the limousine they had just purchased and asking questions about my professional chauffeuring days. While we were talking, I could hear a man in the background; it was the doctor, who had just come into the room. BJ quickly said, "oh, here's the doctor." Then she said goodbye to me and handed the phone to him. I spoke to the doctor for a few minutes about my cousin and the various driving jobs I had previously had. Then I mentioned that I was very interested in meeting them and driving for them. The doctor then asked if I could come to their house the next day so we could take a ride in the limo. I said of course, and then I added that I didn't have a suit any longer. He said, "that doesn't matter; just wear jeans if you want." I said, "great!" The doctor gave me directions to their house, and I told him what time I would be there the next day. It sounded like a great opportunity, and the mysterious element kept me thinking about it. I had always wondered what it would be like to be a private chauffeur, and here was my chance. The only thing that I could relate it to was the television show *Hart to Hart,* and I would finally be playing the part of Max, their driver and butler. We just laughed at the thought as I began to get more and more excited about meeting the Mafioso doctor and his bubbly wife, BJ.

It was the next day, Sunday. I was to be at the doctor's house at 1:00 p.m., so I headed there about forty-five minutes beforehand. As I approached the neighborhood, I noticed the massive homes that lined both sides of the road. These houses were beautifully maintained and had well-manicured grounds. Each house sat off of the road about two hundred feet, and most had driveways that circled around the front of the house. I noticed a few with security gates at the ends of the driveways while I was looking for their address. After a few minutes, I noticed a house that had a white Cadillac stretch limousine sitting in front of it. That had to be the house. As I got closer, I looked at the address to be sure, and I was right. This was the house! It was a beautiful Federal-style, two-story, brick house with a beautiful front yard. I turned into the driveway and began slowly driving toward the house. I looked at the limousine sitting out front, and then I noticed two new cars in the garage. One car was a Rolls Royce Silver Wrath II four door that was a dark metallic green with a tan interior; the other car was a red Mercedes 450 convertible. I thought to myself, *these two do have some money.* I began to get increasingly excited and decided to park my car off to the side of the driveway. At the time, I was driving a Chevy Cavalier, so I felt a little out of place, but I knew that I was going to be driving that huge white Cadillac limousine and that I was going to be a private chauffeur. My excitement grew, and my heart was pounding with the anticipation of meeting both of them. I got out of my car and headed to the front door of the house as I passed by both cars in the garage. As I walked to the front, I looked over the Cadillac limo and looked in the windows. It was white with a red leather interior, and it was enormous. I turned and walked toward the front door of the house to ring the doorbell. I stood there as I heard what sounded like two dogs barking. Then I heard what sounded like someone with high heels walking toward the door. The dogs were barking as the footsteps came closer to the door, and I heard a couple of clicks and then the door opened. To my surprise, it was Marilyn Monroe's double. It was BJ, the doctor's wife, and she was stunning. She was perfectly put together, with blonde hair and an outfit to fit the part. She looked at me, and in the most excited, bubbly tone, she said, "Ric, hi, I'm BJ! Please come in." I walked into the foyer and mentioned to her that she had a beautiful home. It was nice—very nice. Suddenly, the two dogs came from around the corner, both of them very happy to see a new person. These two dogs were all over me, and BJ could barely control them as she introduced me to the dogs. Their names were Cupcake and Moppy-Do. They both had recently been to the groomer and had cute little bows in their hair. It was too funny, as these two dogs were obviously treated as their kids. We laughed at how excited the dogs were to see me, and then BJ said, "they just love you." I laughed and told her they were very cute. As we walked toward the kitchen, she asked if I would like something to drink. I said, "yes, a cola would be great, thank you." BJ poured the soft drink and asked if I would like to see the house. "Of course", I said. Then we walked around the first floor of the finely furnished home. It was beautiful, and the entire first floor had beautiful hardwood floors. The dogs had a blast running and sliding all over the place; they truly had the run of the house. We sat at the kitchen table as BJ talked about herself and their plans to move closer to the city. She mentioned that they were looking at several houses and didn't know which one they would end up bidding on.

It was about ten minutes later when I suddenly heard footsteps coming from the front staircase by the foyer. It was the doctor. As he came around the corner, BJ met him and they hugged and kissed. Then BJ turned toward me, pointed in my direction, and said, "honey, this is Ric." I stood up and walked toward him with my hand extended to shake his. As we were shaking hands and introducing ourselves to each other, BJ was trying to calm down the excited dogs and gain control of them. He was a slightly overweight, handsome, Italian-looking man with a dark tan and coal-black hair that was obviously colored, and not one hair was out of place. He had perfectly manicured fingernails, and his shirt and pants were precisely pressed. He was meticulously put together; it was almost too perfect. He did have that Mafioso look. He said, "Ric, let's sit at the kitchen table." I replied by saying, "great!"

We walked over to the kitchen table and sat down. The doctor asked about my driving record, and I quickly responded by saying, “it’s perfect; not even a traffic ticket.” He thought that was great, and he proceeded to inquire about how long I had driven for the limousine company. I told him that I had driven for them for about six years but that I hadn’t driven for almost two years. He asked if I had experience driving a stretch limousine, because Stella knew only of the Rolls Royce. I told him about the stretch Lincoln limousine that I had driven, and I added that it was the same length as his Cadillac out front. He replied by saying, “good.” Then next topic we discussed was the hourly wage I would want for driving for him. I mentioned that when I worked for the limo company I was paid five dollars an hour. With surprise in his voice, he said, “was that all?” I replied by saying, “yes.” I went on to add that after almost six years I had never received an increase, but I was able to keep all of my tips. “Well that’s good,” he replied as they both laughed. Then he said, “I’ll pay you fifteen dollars an hour to start. How does that sound?” I replied by saying, “that’s great!” I went on and filled them in on the character that was the owner of the limo company, and I told them about the situation that had happened when I decided to quit that job. Both the doctor and BJ were very interested in the stories I told them about driving for the limousine service, and then BJ said, "I bet you have a lot more stories to tell." I replied with a humble yes, thinking to myself that they had no idea what I had been through. They asked where I worked full-time. I proceeded to tell them about my job at the worldwide headquarters of an insurance company. At that time I was a customer service representative for the investments division. It was one of the largest insurance companies. I told them that I did like my job but that I was always looking for advancement opportunities. Then I jokingly said, "who knows, maybe someday you'll need a full-time chauffeur who can cook and clean." They both laughed and replied by saying, "absolutely!"

Then the doctor looked at BJ and then looked at me and said, "do you have time to drive us around today?" I said, "of course." "Let's go for a ride," BJ quickly added. Well, the dogs immediately became so excited that I thought they were going to have heart attacks. The doctor stood up, reached in his pocket, and pulled a set of car keys out and handed them to me. They were the keys to the Cadillac limousine. He then said, "Ric, pull the car around back and we'll lock up." I replied by saying, "yes sir," and then I headed toward the front door, where the limo was. I went out the front door and walked up to the limo. I unlocked the doors and then opened the back doors to check out the passenger quarters. It was beautiful. There was a bar, a television, and room for at least eight people. I got behind the wheel and looked over the dashboard controls. There was also a control panel overhead, and I tried to become acclimated as fast as I possibly could. The limousine had a glass divider that would raise and lower with the click of a switch. This limousine also had a backup battery system. If the car would not start because of a dead battery, all I needed to do was flip a switch to the backup system and we would be all set. When the backup system was activated and in use, it would automatically recharge the main system. The indicator lights on the dash would allow me to tell when the main system was fully recharged so I could flip back over to it. I started the limousine and began to warm up the engine while I waited for them to come out. As I sat there becoming familiar with the controls, I opened the glove compartment to look for the title and insurance papers. I found them, and more. In the glove compartment was a pistol, a .38 special. I grabbed it, and as I was looking at it, I realized that I had just put my fingerprints on it. So I pulled out my handkerchief and wiped it clean. I didn't want my fingerprints on it for anything. I didn't have anything to be worried about, but the thought didn't sit well. I opened the chamber to see if it was loaded. It was—fully loaded and ready to go. The safety wasn't even on! Well, I wiped it clean of my fingerprints and carefully placed it back in the glove compartment. I began to wonder about the things Stella had told me about the doctor being a paranoid Mafioso. Then I had a quick flash of a thought. *What am I getting myself into?* I quickly thought that if I was also going to be a bodyguard, we would need to rethink this hourly rate of $15. That would be on the back burner. Just as I put the gun back, I noticed that the door to the house was opening. So to make them feel as though they had a private chauffeur, I got out of the limo to open the doors so they could get in the back. As I got out of the limo, I noticed that the doctor had his golf clubs and golf shoes. BJ was wearing a sable fur coat. She later told me the make and the cost of the coat. BJ had the dogs on a leash as the doctor locked the house behind them and proceeded to get into the limousine. I put the golf clubs and shoes in the trunk, and after everyone was in the back, I closed the doors and got into the limo and started to pull away. With the glass divider down, I could see and hear everything they were doing and saying. BJ was acting like a giddy little schoolgirl; she was just bubbly and making a fuss over the doctor, saying how good he looked and making comments about him really being rich. It was almost fake, and it was certainly patronizing to him, but I knew my place. I didn't react to any of the comments I heard. Like a professional driver, I merely soaked it all in, and to my surprise, the doctor liked and encouraged that treatment. As we were pulling out of the driveway, I asked the doctor where he would like to go. He replied that he wanted to drive around for a little bit and then hit some golf balls at the nearby driving range. I responded by saying, "yes sir." That "yes sir" always makes them feel like a million dollars, and I knew exactly when to throw that in. Then the doctor spoke up and said, "Ric, there is one thing I need to ask you to do." I said, "sure, what is it?" The doctor replied by saying, "In the glove compartment is a gun. Do you know how to shoot?" I said, "yes, I've seen it, and I have fired a gun just like that." The doctor said, "I need you to carry that with you every time you drive for us. I don't want anyone messing with us." I replied by saying, "Will do." So, after driving around for a while and taking the long way to our destination, I gracefully pulled into the parking lot of the driving range. I found a perfect parking space for the limo—right in front of the doors. The doctor said he needed to put his golf shoes on and asked if I would open the trunk. So I pushed the trunk release and got out of the driver's seat. I opened the door for BJ and the dogs, and then I walked around and opened the doctor's door. I walked back to the trunk and grabbed his golf shoes, placing them in the perfect spot for him. I reached in and grabbed the golf bag out of the trunk and set in on the ground behind the limo. With the trunk lid open, the doctor sat on the back of the limo and began to change his shoes. BJ was talking to the dogs, making the silliest comments to them. She said to the dogs, "Want to watch daddy hit some golf balls? Yes, we're going to watch daddy hit the balls." I just went with the flow not making any comments to her, but just smiling. After the doctor had his golf shoes on, I asked if he wanted me to carry the clubs. He replied by saying, "no, I can handle them." Then BJ spoke up and said, "Ric, I want to watch him hit some golf balls. Would you please take Cupcake and Moppy-Do for a walk so they can pee-pee?" I reluctantly replied by saying, "of course" as she handed over their leashes to me. The doctor and his wife were heading to hit a few balls and I was walking the little girls to go pee-pee. It was a precious moment, and I didn't have a camera; we were a sight to behold.

Everyone on the driving range stopped what they were doing and just stared at us. After the girls did their business, I walked them back to where the doctor and BJ were. Our time at the range lasted about forty-five minutes, and then the doctor became tired of it and decided he wanted to go. I walked to the limo and pushed the trunk release to open the trunk. Just about that time, BJ came over, and I handed her the dog's leashes. The doctor sat on the back of the limo and proceeded to take his shoes off. I assisted by cleaning the grass off of the spikes on the bottom of his shoes and placing them in the trunk while he put his dress shoes back on. I had the back doors to the limo open, and when he finished putting his shoes on, he proceeded to get in the back seat. I placed the golf clubs in the trunk, closed it, and then closed the back doors of the limo. I got into the limo and started the engine, put the gear into drive, and began to pull away. As I did so, I could hear BJ making a fuss over the doctor again. She was telling him how good of a golfer he was and how he had really hit the balls far. She told him how good he looked several times.

I thought, *does she always act like this? Does she constantly make a fuss over him?* I quickly realized her duty; she was there to make him feel good. After making our appearance at the driving range to show off the limousine for the doctor, we headed back to their house. During the entire trip, BJ was constantly talking about how good he looked and how well he hit the balls. It was sickening. We soon arrived at the house, and as I pulled into the driveway, the doctor said that I didn't need to pull the car around the front of the house, so I parked the limo by my car. As we pulled beside my car, I made a joke about it and asked the doctor if he wanted to trade cars, telling him that I could take that little red Mercedes and he could have my Cavalier. We all laughed, as he knew I wasn't serious, but if he had said yes, I would have taken that Mercedes convertible in a second. I stopped the limo and got out to open their doors, asking the doctor if he wanted me to take the golf clubs and shoes into the house for him. He replied by saying, "no, I would like you to put them in the Rolls if you would." I responded with a "yes sir" as he handed me the keys to his Rolls Royce and asked me to pull it out of the garage for him. He was planning to go into the office to do some paperwork. I again responded with a "yes sir." I put the golf bag and shoes in the trunk of the Rolls Royce and got behind the wheel. The door closed with a solid, quiet sound I wasn't used to, and as I noticed the distinct smell of leather and felt the cushiony, comfortable seats, I had to stop for a moment and bask in my glory. It was like heaven! I started the Rolls Royce without hearing a sound from the engine. The inside of that car was so quiet that I had to look at the gages on the dashboard to make sure it had started. Then I moved the gearshift into reverse to back up. There was no jolt of the transmission going into gear, so I lightly tapped on the gas pedal, and that car just floated smoothly as I backed out of the garage. It was like no other car I had driven. It was newer than the Rolls Royces I had driven for the limo company, and it had been well maintained. It was like floating on a cloud. I parked the car where the doctor wanted it, and then I locked it and headed toward the house. When I walked into the kitchen, BJ and the doctor were sitting at the kitchen table. The doctor had his checkbook out and was writing a check as BJ was sitting there talking about what a good driver I was. She loved riding in that Cadillac, and now she had a private driver, and she mentioned that she could hardly wait until the next time I came to drive. She sounded as though she was already making plans. The doctor finished writing the check and pulled it from the checkbook and handed it to me. We had been driving for four hours, which would have been a total of $60. When I looked at the check,

I noticed it was written for $350. He quickly said, "buy yourself a new suit." I said, "thank you, I will." They thanked me again, and I said, "I'm looking forward to working for you. Please give me a call whenever you need me." They said they would do just that.

I couldn't wait to get home and tell everyone I knew about the private driving job I had just landed. I was very excited, and I felt that this was my golden opportunity. Everyone I told seemed to be envious and had a lot of questions about the doctor and his wife. This was going to be a fun job.

Before I'd had a chance to drive for them again, BJ called one evening. She was very excited, and she said they had bought a house in town so the doctor wouldn't have to drive so far to work. When she told me where it was, I knew the exact house, as I had grown up very close to it.

The next week, I received a call at work from BJ. She wanted to know if I was interested in helping her unpack some boxes at the new house. I said, "of course." We planned to unpack and arrange furniture, as she mentioned that she needed some suggestions, and then she said, "now, you know we're going to pay you for this, too." I replied by saying, "great."

It was a beautiful four-bedroom house with the master suite on the first floor. There was an attached four-car garage and a tennis court on the huge corner lot. We spent a total of about two weeks unpacking boxes, hanging pictures and rearranging furniture. That woman saved everything and didn't want to throw anything away. We were unpacking some pictures when I saw a large photo of her, the doctor, and President Regan at the White House. When I inquired about it, BJ was all too happy to explain. The doctor had received an award for his accomplishments as a heart surgeon and for being on the team that had helped develop the balloon procedure that expands arteries. I was very impressed; that must have been an honor. Later that evening, we unpacked clothes—box after box of clothes. Then it was shoes—boxes and boxes of shoes. There must have been at least eighty pairs of shoes. There were so many clothes and shoes that we designated one bedroom as her closet and dressing room. The bedroom directly across the hall was being turned into her hair salon. I mean, this woman had purchased salon-grade sinks and hair dryers. BJ also ordered a stackable washer and dryer so she didn't have to take the towels downstairs to the laundry. It was truly amazing. BJ then asked if I could take a few bags of clothes to the Salvation Army, which I quickly agreed to do. She didn't need to hang on to that old stuff. We were just about done unpacking the last of the boxes when the phone rang. BJ had left the cordless phone somewhere in the house and couldn't find it, so she had to run downstairs to answer it. I was looking through a huge box of papers when I ran across some letters. I started to read them, as any normal curious human would. They were letters from her girlfriends, and I mean close girlfriends. One letter I read made me think that BJ was a bit unstable, and it mentioned that she had been irrational in a phone conversation the two had had at one point. I soon realized that BJ might have gone off the deep end at one point, as the letter mentioned a short stay at a hospital and her friend mentioned that she was glad that she had helped her. I wish I could have read more, but time didn't allow. I could hear her side of the conversation on the phone call, and then she said goodbye and hung up. I quickly put the letters I was reading on the bottom of the pile as BJ came back up to the bedroom where we were unpacking. We were unpacking the last box when she noticed it had some letters in the bottom. She grabbed them so as to not let me see them, and she put them in a desk that was in the bedroom. I acted like I didn't even notice what she grabbed, and I began to take the empty boxes downstairs to take them to the trash. When I came back upstairs, I could tell that she had been looking at the letters while I was taking the trash out. She looked as though she had been crying, and she was trying to pull herself together so I wouldn't notice. I went along acting as though noting was wrong, but I wanted to change the mood, so I asked her how she had met the doctor. Well, that was all I needed to ask, she didn't stop talking for forty-five minutes. She said that she was living in Las Vegas when she met him. She was a beautician and manicurist, and he came into the shop. Among the papers I found was an expired Nevada driver's license, so I knew she was telling me the truth. She didn't go into much more detail about Las Vegas, but she said that she was on a diet when she married the doctor. She said it almost killed her. In fact, the doctor was going to divorce her if she didn't get off of it. He told her that the ingredients were making her insane and would eventually kill her, so she stopped taking the supplements. The best thing about working for this couple was that the doctor wasn't around much of the time. He always had the strangest hours for someone in his position. He could have named his own hours, and yet he decided to work late into the evening on many occasions. He would often call the house when I was there to talk specifically to me. I felt that I served as BJ's bodyguard, babysitter, and entertainer. It seemed to satisfy him when I was at the house, and if I was there, he knew that she wouldn't be cheating on him. It was really odd. I would get on the phone, and we really didn't talk about much, so it seemed pointless to me, but I obliged. I often thought he didn't trust her.

Because we were so close in age, BJ and I hit it off quickly, and we soon had all of the unpacking and rearranging of furniture done. She mentioned that she wanted to go to the mall on the following Saturday around 3:00 p.m. to do some shopping, and she wanted me to drive her in the limo. I said I would be there by 2:00 p.m. to wash the limo and then get dressed in time for us to leave at three. She thought that was great and said she was looking forward to it.

The following Saturday, I arrived at 1:30 p.m. in the afternoon to wash the limo. The house had a four-car garage attached, but it wasn't enough for his collection. He was building a six-car garage on the property to house five cars. One was the limo, so the garage was being built so that you could park one car in front of another. That way the limo could take up two spaces. BJ had told me that his cars were being stored in a hangar and would be delivered in a couple of weeks. He had a couple of T-Birds, a Corvette, and an MG. She said, "Ric, you're going to love his cars."

I arrived and started into the house to take my clothes up to the extra bedroom so that I could shower, change, and be ready for her shopping trip after washing the limo. I opened the front door, and BJ was dancing to the jukebox in the entry hall. She had an old jukebox that had a fairly old selection of tunes, but it was fun. All you had to do was punch the numbers and it would play. How much fun is that? I laughed as I passed her dancing with the dogs, and I took my clothes up to the bedroom and then went out to wash the limo. It was fun washing the limo, as the house was on a corner lot at a pretty busy intersection. Of course, everyone that stopped for the traffic light watched as I was washing the limo. There were always those that would yell out of their cars, "is my car next?" I would just laugh and wave at them. I finished the limo and went in to take a shower and change into my tuxedo. When I was ready, I took my old clothes out to my car and started the limo to cool it down, as it was a warm day and I was in a black suit. After a few minutes, I looked at my watch. It was 3:00 p.m. Not a minute later, the front door opened, and I couldn't believe my eyes. She looked like a million dollars. Of course, she had a million dollars, and when you have that kind of money, it's easy to look good. I opened the door for her to get in, and she was very happy. Her private driver was taking her to go shopping. I just loved it! I got behind the wheel and we headed out of the driveway. I asked her which entrance of the mall she wanted to be dropped off at, and she quickly told me the store she wanted to go to. I pulled up in front of the store and got out of the car. I walked around to her door and opened it as people were stopping and staring. BJ loved anyone that would make a fuss over her, and I was playing it up (and doing a great job, too). I gave her my phone number and told her to give me a fifteen-minute lead before she came out of the store. That way I would be there waiting to open the door for her. She thought that was great, and she headed into the store as I headed to my house to wait for her call. I had been home for about two hours when the phone rang; it was BJ, and she was ready to go. I asked where she wanted me to pick her up, and she told me she wanted me to go to the loading dock. I said, "the loading dock?" She said, "yes Ric, I bought a coffee table and two end tables. They're beautiful, and you're going to love them." I told her I would be there in less than fifteen-minutes, and I headed to the mall.

The furniture she bought was the heaviest furniture I have ever had to lift. Each piece had a marble top, and we had to get them in the back of the limo. So, with the help of two employees of the store, we managed. They took up all of the room in the back of the limo, and BJ had to ride up front with me. It was hilarious! While she was sitting up front, she talked about the garage that was being built. I mentioned how nice it would be not to have to wash the cars every other day. Then I asked her about his cars. She said, "Oh Ric, they are beautiful." Then she went on to tell me about each car. In addition to the Cadillac limo, Mercedes 450 coupe, Rolls Royce Silver Wrath II, and the Lincoln Continental that BJ usually drove, the cars that were being delivered were a 1954 MG Convertible, a 1956 white Thunderbird, a 1957 powder blue Thunderbird, a 1958 Mercedes coupe, and a 1963 red Corvette convertible. All I could say was that I was very happy for a garage!

I drove BJ on many shopping excursions and witnessed her spending thousands of dollars. It was unbelievable to me how someone could just throw money around without a care in the world. I mean, she didn't even flinch, and I enjoyed watching her do it.

One of the things that the doctor got a kick out of was putting on a show and being the big shot. He always liked showing off and flaunting his money and status. There were times when I knew this and would put on a show for him. I drove them to dinner a lot, and every time I would be out front waiting on them I would have people walking up to the car, wanting to look inside, and even asking to sit in it.

When I worked for the limo company this was not a problem as long as the people weren't drunk. But in this case it was a private car, and I never let anyone get in the back. I rather enjoyed telling people that it was a private car and that I was their personal chauffeur. It left many people speechless.

By this point in my private driving career, I had overheard many conversations between the doctor and BJ. He became increasingly rude and mean to her. He would always demand that everything go his way. He was like a little, rich, selfish brat. I remember one particular evening on which I was scheduled to drive them to dinner. I was standing in the game room, which was where his desk was, and he was writing out some bills. We were all ready, but the doctor was taking his time writing out the bills when their conversation took a turn. That's when I decided to leave the room, but I heard the whole argument from the restroom, and then I heard what sounded like him slapping her. Then I heard him calling her all kinds of names. He was very verbally abusive to her, but she put up with it. After all, that was her meal ticket, and he could cut it off, leaving her nothing. So every time they argued, she quickly gave in to him. I think it was out of fear of being beaten. When I thought it was okay to come out of the bathroom, I headed to the game room and caught a glimpse of her face. One side of her face was red, so he probably had slapped her. I didn't see it, but I heard it. I didn't dare mention a word of it, or I would be out of a job. I continued to stand there while he finished writing the bills, and then I heard him say to me, "take these letters out to the mailbox." I looked at him, and in his hand were about fifteen envelopes ready to be mailed. I couldn't figure out why he wanted me to put them in the mailbox, as it was Saturday evening after the mail had come. Thinking I was doing him a favor, I said, "I can drop these at the post office on my way home." With a loud growl, he said, "no, I asked you to put them in the mailbox . . . out front . . . right now . . . what's the matter with you, didn't you hear me?" Well, that was the turning point in our relationship. I had witnessed his abuse of his wife, and now he was angry with me for no valid reason. All I wanted to do was a favor for him, and I was bitten. I had never seen him snap like that. Needless to say, I turned around and headed for the door, saying that I would be waiting out front with the limo, and I took those letters out to the mailbox. The rest of that evening was like walking on pins and needles. Every time BJ opened her mouth, she spoke quietly and he still snapped at her. Me? I didn't say much the rest of the evening. I only spoke when he spoke to me. I didn't have anything to say to him; he had really pissed me off, and I couldn't wait to take them home.

Several days went by before I received a call from them. Usually BJ would call and speak in a high-pitched squeal, saying "Hi Ric, can you drive this Saturday?" I never turned them down because it was good money and because it was fun most of the time. They did want me to drive them to the football game on the upcoming Saturday. These games were a big deal in town; in fact, not much else went on when there was a football game. They informed me that we would be going to Stella's restaurant, where she and her husband were going to the game with four others in the limo.

Game day came, and they had the limo packed with booze. We headed off to the restaurant, which was close to the stadium. When we arrived at the restaurant, everyone was ready to get into the limo, and they all started guzzling the doctor's booze. It took about ten minutes to get to the stadium, and as you can imagine, they were all tanked. I dropped them off and found a spot to park where the doctor knew I would be.

By the beginning of the fourth quarter, the home team was losing pretty badly, and there was no winning game that day. I soon saw all of them walking toward the limo, and as each of them got in the back, I knew they were ready to go home. No one was in a good mood at all. When we arrived at the restaurant, the doctor and BJ didn't want to go in. I thought that to be odd, because they always liked Stella's restaurant. She gave them free food and treated them well. BJ told Stella that they were tired and wanted to go home. They said their goodbyes, and we began to pull away. We didn't even get out of the driveway of the restaurant before the doctor started to refer to Stella as "that bitch." I almost choked on air. I couldn't believe my ears. Then the doctor said, "I'm sorry she is your cousin, but she is a real B-I-T-C-H!" Well the only response I had was to say, "she's really something, isn't she?"

Apparently he had good reason to be pissed at her. Something had happened at the stadium that I hadn't heard about. I do know that the entire time I was driving the limo, Stella was constantly telling me what to do and how to drive. I was almost ready to hit her and was about to drag her out of the window myself. I wouldn't exactly have called her a bitch, but there was also a liquor factor, and that may have been why the doctor hadn't gotten his way. I also realized that the doctor and BJ often talked behind the backs of those that they had just had dinner with. They would get into the limo after dinner and just talk about everyone that was at the table. I think it must have made them feel good. I really don't know, but it made me wonder what they said about me. We arrived back at their house, and I got out of the limo to open the doors for them to get out of the back. As they headed into the house, the doctor asked me to come inside after I put the limo in the garage. I said okay, got in the limo, and then pulled into the garage. As I entered the house, I could hear them talking and laughing about Stella. I just started laughing, and we joked about her telling me how to drive. I was putting the gun back into the cabinet as I did after every driving job, and the doctor was writing out a check for me as he usually did at the end of the evening. BJ spoke up and asked what I was doing on the next Sunday afternoon. I answered by saying, "I have nothing planned. Do you need me to drive?" She said, "yes, I have a family reunion to go to." I said, "of course." The doctor had no interest in seeing or spending any time with those "hillbillies" as he referred to them. She told me the name of the town, and it was about ninety minutes away. She said that we were going to be there for a few hours, and then she mentioned that her grandmother would be coming back with us. I told her that it would be fun for grandma to ride in the limo, and I said I would see them the next week.

Sunday came around, and I had my tux and a change of clothes with me. BJ said that I could change into shorts after we got there, but she wanted them all to see me in my suit first. We filled up the fridge in the limo with bottles of water and several cans of soda. I also stopped at the gas station to fill the tank up prior to getting on the freeway. We were on the highway, and BJ was in a talkative mood. She started to tell me about all of the relatives. Hearing some of the stories made me wonder why I was in a tux. We exited the freeway to go to her grandma's house to pick her up before the reunion. Grandma's eyesight was terrible. I don't even think she knew what kind of car we were riding in. All she knew is that it was a big white car. We headed to the state park where the family reunion was, and we pulled into the picnic area, which had a shelter house. There were only about five or six cars there, and the kids came running up to the limo as we approached. I got out of the car and opened the doors for BJ and her grandmother to get out. Well, I don't think there were twenty teeth in the entire crowd, but everyone was very nice. I felt so out of place that I grabbed my clothes and went to the restroom to change. I put my tux in the trunk of the car and headed to the beer cooler for a cold one. One of BJ's nephews came over to me and introduced himself. He was very nice, and I stood around talking to him most of the time I was there. The food soon was ready, so we went over and indulged. Another of BJ's nephews came over and started chatting with me and asked if I had ever seen her in a porno magazine. I was shocked. I said, "what? BJ?" He said, "yes." I couldn't believe what I was hearing. He continued on, telling me the name and specific issue of the magazine and describing her pose. I couldn't wait to get home and try to find that magazine.

We had probably been there for about two hours when BJ came over and told me that she was ready to return home. We had a long drive, and her granny was anxious to get to town. After saying our goodbyes, we all loaded into the limo and headed to the highway. We had been on the freeway for about thirty minutes when I heard a fluttering noise coming from the back seat, where BJ and granny were. I suddenly realized what that noise was. It was granny, and she had bad, bad, gas. At the same time I noticed it, BJ yelled, "Oh my God, what is that?" It was a toxic cloud, and I tried to keep a straight face. By this time BJ was lowering the windows in the back, and I was lowering them up front and opening the sunroof. I spoke up and said, "must have been a skunk." We continued on the freeway, and after about twenty minutes, I noticed that traffic was slowing and backing up. Suddenly, traffic was stopped. We sat in one spot for about five minutes, so we were thinking that there was an accident. Then, as traffic began to creep slowly forward, granny mentioned that she had to go to the bathroom. I thought to myself, *didn't you just go?* So there we were, traveling about five miles an hour while granny had to go to the bathroom, and there was no rest area in sight. As the freeway curved, I noticed that the backup was the work of two tractor-trailers traveling about five miles per hour side by side, blocking both lanes and swerving to cut off anyone that was trying to get around them. I couldn't believe it. Granny had to go, and I needed to get around those two trucks. So I carefully started driving down the emergency lane with my emergency flashers on. These two trucks were running to the edge of the freeway and wouldn't let anyone by them. But granny had to go, and I wasn't about to clean that mess on the back seat. I knew I had to get by them, so I cautiously approached the semi that was in the right lane. He could clearly see that I was driving a limo, and I had my emergency flashers on, but that didn't stop him. Just as the limo's front end was even with the semi's back end, the driver swerved to the right, succeeding in running us off of the freeway. Luckily we were only traveling about fifteen miles per hour, so I went off of the road and into the grass, barely missing the reflective sign, with granny and BJ screaming in the back seat. I didn't want the back end of the limo to swing around; if it did, we would be stuck. So I punched the gas as we were bouncing along in the grass, and I soon noticed that I was ahead of the truck. I quickly pulled back onto the freeway and looked in the rearview mirror in time to see the truck driver giving me the middle finger. BJ was cussing like a sailor as I opened my window and returned the gesture. I looked again in the rearview mirror, and

I noticed that BJ had her gun out and was looking back at the truck, which was getting smaller as we accelerated away. BJ said, "Ric, you're a regular James Bond. Thank you for saving our lives." I only responded by saying, "Granny's got to go, and I'll get her there." Then I said, "BJ, you can put your gun away now." She just laughed; she had been ready to blow him away. I quickly headed down the freeway to find a bathroom, and I soon came upon several restaurants. I pulled in and let BJ and granny out. After about fifteen minutes, they both came out to the car. We jumped back on the highway and headed home without incident. When we arrived, BJ was telling the doctor about my driving abilities, and he couldn't believe what had happened. He was very appreciative and gave me an extra hundred dollars. I collected my check and said goodbye; I needed to shower and relax after that.

Over the next few months, I drove for the doctor and BJ several times. He also had several meetings which he was expected to attend, and I was always ready whenever they would call.

Then next call came when BJ wanted to invite us to the doctor's birthday cookout. She wanted to be sure that we came, and she said we would have a day of fun with no work. We could play tennis and just relax. We arrived early for the birthday party, and I asked if there was anything we could do to help. My partner was with me, and it seemed that BJ had spent all morning on herself and not the party. We gathered up the soda cans and began to prepare the burgers. The doctor was wandering around the back yard, walking the dogs. The entire setting was strange. BJ went out to talk to the doctor, and I got the impression that he was mad or that they had been arguing again. Well, the doctor became increasingly irritated, as it was now forty-five minutes past the time on the invitation and we were the only ones there. He stormed into the kitchen and slammed a book on the counter. He was pissed. No one was coming to his party. The doctor went into his bedroom with BJ on his heels, and then the door slammed shut. I looked at my partner, and we just laughed at how childish he was acting. I asked him if he wanted to leave. He said, "no way." A few minutes later, the doorbell rang. There were other guests arriving, and one couple was my cousin Stella and her husband. She looked at my partner and me and said, "what are you doing here?" I responded by saying, "we were invited, and we were on time." She is a character larger than life. What a piece of work! We stayed at the birthday party cookout for about an hour longer and then decided to leave. The doctor was very embarrassed after the way he had acted, like a little selfish brat pouting at his birthday party. It was a strange afternoon, and you could say we had enough, and Stella didn't help.

That next week while I was at work, I received a call from BJ saying that they were planning a trip to California. They were going to be gone ten days, and they wanted to know if I would take care of the dogs and stay at the house. I told her that I would be glad to, but I told her that I did have to work, so I would need to run home at lunch and let the dogs out for a break and then return in the evening after work. She thought that would be fine and asked me to come over that evening to talk about the details.

When I arrived at their house and walked in, I couldn't believe what a good mood the doctor was in. I became accustomed to entering the house and waiting to see what kind of mood he was in. This particular night he was in a good mood, and he wouldn't stop talking. He was actually rather pleasant and acting very civil. It was odd behavior for him; he was usually going off about something, but not on this evening. We sat at the kitchen table and had a few drinks while we talked about their trip to Carmel, California. The doctor owned a condo there, and he was going out to talk to a realtor about listing it. Apparently it was for sale, but he said he wanted to light a fire under the realtor's butt, because in his mind there wasn't much interest in it, and he didn't think that the realtor was doing a good enough job.

They were going to be leaving on a Thursday evening and returning a week later on a Sunday afternoon. They asked me to take them to the airport in the limo and also to pick them up when they returned. I would also be taking the dogs to their weekly grooming appointment, which wasn't a problem. I was going to be staying at their house and would have access to all of their cars, and it sounded like fun.

I took that Thursday off as a vacation day and arrived well ahead of the time they wanted to leave for the airport. Of course, the dogs had to ride to the airport in the limo and say goodbye too. I dropped the doctor and BJ off at the departing flight counter, and we agreed that I would pick them up at the arriving flight doors. They said that they would have a skycap take care of the luggage, so all I needed to do was meet them at the curb. After saying our goodbyes I headed back to their house with the dogs; they were having a great time playing in the back of the limo, as it was almost as comfortable to them as their home was. We arrived at the house, and I opened the garage door and backed the limo into its usual spot, right next to the two thunderbirds, which were next to the '63 Corvette and the '54 MG. It was a fun job at times.

I let the dogs in the house and then went to my car to get my clothes. I took my clothes into the master bedroom closet and arranged them in a spot that had been cleared for me. The master bedroom was really cool. As you walked in, the bathroom area, which contained the spa tub, shower, bathtub, and double sinks, was off to the left. To the right was the huge closet and the hallway to the bedroom. On the other side of the bed was a hallway that passed another closet and then entered the same bathroom area. There were windows all around, and you could look out into the backyard and tennis court. It was a pretty nice layout, and of course it was well decorated.

I had finished unpacking my clothes, and I decided to crack open a beer and play with the dogs for a while. I felt a bit uneasy in that big house, and I walked around, checking all of the windows and doors to make sure they were locked. They didn't have an alarm system, but there were guns all over that house, and each one was loaded and ready to use.

I found a gun under the bed, one in the master bedroom closet, one under the couch in the living room, and even one in the bathroom. That house came complete with an arsenal. One plus was that the liquor cabinet was packed to the gills. I could make any drink that I could think of.

I stayed the weekend and had to go to work on Monday morning as usual. When I arrived at work, I decided to take Thursday and Friday off as well. I asked my supervisor, and he said it would be fine. By this time, everyone that I worked with knew all about the doctor, BJ, and the dogs, and they got a kick out of hearing of their escapades. I hadn't been at work two hours when the phone rang; it was the doctor calling from California. He wanted to know how the dogs were, and he asked if I was going to go home at lunch to check on them. I assured him that the dogs had plenty of food and water and that yes, I would be taking a long lunch to go and check on them.

Tuesday evening, while I was walking the dogs around the yard at the house, I heard the phone ringing. I ran in to the house to get it, and it stopped ringing just as I reached for it. I just knew it was the doctor calling, but I didn't have a phone number for them in California. The phone had been disconnected at the condo because no one was living there. This was also during the time when cell phones had not reached the popularity of today.

Later that evening, while I was in the shower, I heard the phone ringing. I jumped out of the shower to pick it up, and it stopped just as I got to it.

The next day, while I was at work, the doctor called and proceeded to accuse me of not being at the house. He said he had called twice and I hadn't answered. I explained that I did hear the phone when I was in the backyard walking the dogs and while in the shower. I told him that I had gone for the phone both times and that it had stopped ringing just as I had gotten to it. That didn't matter to him; he still had an attitude. So, using a tactic that BJ used, I quickly changed the subject and talked about something else. That worked for her, and to my disbelief, it worked for me.

I told the doctor that I would be taking two vacation days that week and would be at the house from Thursday until I would leave to pick them up at the airport on Sunday. He thought that was a good idea, and after chatting for another few minutes, we hung up. I was very nice to him, but it was one of those times that as soon as I hung up the phone, I had a few choice words for him.

I stayed at the house from Thursday on, and when Saturday came, it was time to take the dogs to the groomer to get their weekly ribbons in their hair. What a sight! I took them out to the limo and we headed for the groomer. I pulled that limo right in front of the dog groomer's shop, got out and opened the back door for them. I grabbed their leashes and we walked into the shop. Everyone there knew the two dogs, and the dogs were excited to see everyone.

I asked the owner how long they would be there and what time I needed to return to pick them up. I had two hours to waste, so I went back to the house and watched a little football on the television.

While I was sitting there, I decided to do a little cleaning in preparation for their return. My partner had arrived and decided to help. We went through that entire house, cleaning windows, blinds, and bathrooms and running the sweeper. I was getting paid for that as well, and as you might have guessed, BJ couldn't keep a housekeeper.

I had told her about a friend that had a housekeeper named Garnet. Garnet was a wild character, and she cleaned houses as a profession. She had a small, dedicated client list, and I didn't even know if she would be able to fit them into her schedule. I called Garnet, and she agreed to meet them. On the first day that Garnet arrived to work for them, she apparently parked on the freshly paved part of the driveway that had been added. Garnet didn't know not to; there wasn't any caution tape blocking it. All she knew was that it was an area away from the front doors.

BJ saw her pull onto the fresh blacktop and came flying out of the house, screaming at Garnet and swearing like a sailor. The doctor wasn't home, and BJ told Garnet that he was going to be very upset and that he would blame her for letting Garnet park her car there. BJ called me at home in a frantic frenzy. BJ kept saying, "he's going to kill me." If she said it once, she said it twenty times. I told her to hang on and said that I would be there in about fifteen minutes. When I arrived, I saw nothing that would make me think that Garnet had ruined the driveway. I assured BJ that the doctor probably wouldn't even notice it unless she pointed it out to him. I could see tire tracks, but there was nothing close to what she had described over the phone.

Shortly after I arrived, Garnet came out of the door. She looked at me and rolled her eyes, not letting BJ see the disgust on her face.

After BJ went into the house, Garnet said to me, "Ric, thank you for the lead, but this isn't going to work out." I told Garnet that I totally understood. Garnet went on to tell me that BJ had watched every move she made in the house like a hawk while telling her what to do and how to do it. Garnet told me that this would be the last day she would be there as she said, "I don't need this shit." I just laughed and told her that I understood.

The phone rang and I picked it up. It was the dog groomer calling to say they had finished early, so I locked the house up and headed over to pick up the dogs. They were so happy to see me; they were so cute with their little ribbons in their hair. I put them into the back of the limo and we headed home. They were happy to get home, and of course they searched the house, thinking that BJ and the doctor would be there.

Sunday rolled around, and it was time to head to the airport to pick up BJ and the doctor. I had gathered up my clothes and put them in my car. I made a sweep of the house to make sure everything was in place and then headed to the airport.

I arrived at the airport flight arrival door and didn't see anyone, so I circled around again, looking at the other exits and thinking they were confused about where I was going to pick them up. I must have circled five or six times when I saw BJ standing by herself at the curb. I pulled over and got out of the limo. She didn't have any luggage with her and looked as though she was upset. When I got out of the car, BJ said, "where the hell have you been? The doctor is pissed."

I told her that we had agreed on meeting at the arriving flight doors, which was where I had been sitting. "I had decided to drive around to check the other exits when I saw you standing here," I said. BJ told me where the doctor was waiting, and we got into the limo and headed in that direction. I quickly headed to where he was, standing at the taxi stand. That was not where we agreed on meeting, because I knew I wouldn't be able to sit there and wait for them to come out.

I stopped the car and got out to put the luggage in the trunk. He had a look on his face like that of a little fat boy that was lost and had been pouting. He was even limping as if he was in pain or to gain sympathy or something. He looked pitiful and acted the same.

Of course, when I got out of the limo his first response was, "where the hell were you?"

I replied by saying, "where we agreed to meet, at the arriving flights door." I then pointed to the sign above his head that read "TAXI WAITING ONLY" and said, "this is not arriving flights, it's on the next level."

Well, he looked at the sign and realized that he was wrong. Did he admit it? No. He went on about how long he had been standing there, and he didn't even acknowledge that this whole situation was his fault. Nothing was ever his fault.

Well, you can imagine that it was a quiet ride home that day. I'm sure they were cussing me in the back seat of that limo, since the first thing he did when he got in was raise the glass divider so he didn't have to talk to me and so I couldn't converse with them. He acted like a little brat!!

When we arrived at the house, I pulled up to the front door. I got out to open the doors, and he had already opened his own door to get out. I opened the door for BJ and she at least thanked me. He said nothing as I carried the luggage into the house to put it on the beds in the master bedroom so they could unpack. After all of the luggage was in, I walked by them and said I would put the limo away and be right back.

When I came back into the house, I saw the doctor sitting at his desk in the game room, looking through the stack of mail. He was not writing a check as he usually did. Instead, BJ turned to me and said that they were tired and that they would figure out my pay sometime later that week. I sensed that I was not going to be paid for my service, but

I knew they were upset. They were upset at their mistake, but they never saw it that way.

They always would find fault in the work that anyone did at their house in an effort to get a discount or even to refuse to pay in some cases.

I remember a landscaper that planted flowers and bushes for them. After he was completely done, he asked for his check. They suddenly refused to pay him, saying that everything had been planted in the wrong spots and that the plants were dying. I saw the plans, and he had done exactly what they wanted him to do. The landscaper had even reminded them to water the plants if they were not going to install a sprinkler system.

Shortly after that argument, while I was washing one of the cars, the landscaper pulled up in his truck with a crew of four, and they began pulling flowers and bushes out of the ground and tossing them in the back of the pickup truck. I didn't stop them; I just laughed. He walked by me at one point and said, "if they're not going to pay me, I will repossess my plants."

He didn't care if they were dead; all of them came out of the ground, and he left huge holes where every plant and bush had been. It was rather humorous. Suddenly, BJ came running out of the house, asking what the hell they were doing. I replied by saying, “the landscaper said you didn’t pay the bill, so he is repossessing his plants.”

That next day I called to ask BJ about the check. She said that she was going to mail it to me. I replied by saying, “okay.”

Then I mentioned a job that they had already asked me to do the next week. She said that they were canceling that because the doctor wasn’t feeling well.

Three days later, I received a check in the mail for $100. It was about $400 short, so I called her to let her know that the check was wrong. BJ replied by saying, “I know.”

I said, “that’s all you’re going to pay me is $100?” Then I went on to say, “I took three days of vacation, took those dogs to the groomer, sat at that house every night, cleaned for two days straight, and you’re only paying me $100?

BJ replied in the calmest voice, saying, “if you’re not happy with the check, you can send it back, but that’s all we’re going to pay you.”

In the calmest voice, I responded by saying, “you ungrateful bastards.” Then I slammed the phone down. I jumped in my car and went to a branch of their bank and cashed that check immediately before they could stop payment on it.

Needless to say, I never heard from them again. I had been a loyal and dedicated employee, and they had turned on me. I had done everything they had asked me to do. On one occasion the doctor asked me to take the limo to a dealership to have some bodywork done.

One day he had decided to pull the limo out and take it for a ride. He had to have BJ watch as he moved it though the driveway. She did a great job of guiding him right into a stone retaining wall, scratching and denting the side door.

When I went to pick up the car, I got in and put the key in the ignition. Nothing happened, not even a click. The batteries were dead, even the backup battery. So I manually unlocked the doors and opened the back to see what was wrong. I noticed that the carpets were all out of place; it appeared as though someone had been in the back. I looked in the little trashcan and saw an empty fast food bag. I noticed that an ashtray was left open on the door. As I looked in the ashtray, I noticed a couple of cigarette butts, and upon a closer look, I noticed the remains of a marijuana cigarette. Someone had been partying in the back of the limo and had left the stereo on, which was why both batteries were drained.

Then I suddenly remembered that I had set the trip odometer, and I went to the driver's seat to check it. Fifty-four miles had been added to the odometer. Not only had they partied, but they had also gone for a joyride.

I went back into the dealership and asked for the manager. When he came to the front, I told him about the dead batteries, the carpets, and the ashtray contents. I told him that I had to call the doctor and tell him because he was expecting the limo to be home that evening.

I used the phone at the front desk, and as I was talking to the doctor, everyone was listening, and I knew that the doctor would be highly upset. The doctor told me to go ahead and leave, but he had me hand the phone to the manager before I left.

The manager picked up the phone and didn't say anything for about two minutes. Then he apologized again and again, promising to take care of the situation.

The dealership delivered the limo the next day with two new batteries and an invoice that said "NO CHARGE."

Two months after my last conversation with the doctor and BJ, I was writing Christmas cards when I ran across their names in my address book. I suddenly had flashbacks of all of my hard work and dedication that had barely been rewarded. I decided to send them a card without a return address so they wouldn't throw it away without opening it. Inside the card I wrote a simple line: "I hope you're happy, Merry Christmas."

It was now two months later, a cold February day, and I was sitting at my desk, working for the insurance company. My phone rang, and I saw on the caller readout that it was my mother calling. She often called to chat or relay gossip from the neighborhood or ask me to look up a phone number for her. So, thinking this was going to be one of her usual calls, I prepared myself and answered the phone. We chatted for a few minutes then she said, "your buddy is in the paper." I replied by saying, "my buddy, who?" She answered, saying, "your doctor friend." I said, "Really? what for?" thinking that he had been given another award or that there was some type of article about his accomplishments. Mom replied by saying, "he's in the obituary!" I couldn't believe what I was hearing. I asked her if it gave any indication as to how he had died and she said it did not; it just said that he had died suddenly at home.

Well, I told my mother that I had to go find a newspaper. I would call her back later that day. I said goodbye to her and hung up. I turned to the associates in my immediate work area and told them what my mother had said. They couldn't believe it either.

I finally found a newspaper and quickly searched for the obituaries. Soon I found it and read the entire write-up. It merely said that he had died suddenly at home, and that was it. I had a feeling that there was more to it, and I decided to call their house.

While the phone was ringing and I was waiting for someone to pick up, I had a flash of thought about how rich BJ was going to be with all of those restored vehicles and that house. She would be worth millions.

Suddenly, someone picked up the phone. I could tell immediately that it was not BJ, so I introduced myself. The woman that answered the phone was BJ's aunt, whom I had met at the family reunion.

I asked her to give my condolences to BJ and then said, "I had no idea that he was sick."

BJ's aunt replied by saying, "neither did anyone else."

I asked her to let BJ know that I would see her at the funeral home, and then I hung up the phone.

When my partner and I went to the funeral home two nights later, we walked in and saw the doctor laid out in the casket. There were only about fifteen people there, and maybe four or five bouquets of flowers.

I recognized the doctor's two sons, and I gave them my condolences as I introduced myself and shook their hands. I noticed that BJ was walking around the funeral parlor with a video camera, taking videos of the flowers and of the doctor in the casket. I thought that was very odd thing to do. I had never seen that before, and I thought about how morbid it was. *Who in their right mind would want that video?* I thought to myself.

When she put the video camera down, I walked over to her and gave her a hug. I remembered my last conversation with her had ended with me calling them ungrateful bastards and hanging up, so I didn't know how well I would be received.

She said hi and thanked us for coming as we hugged. I told her that I didn't even know that he was sick, and I asked what had happened. She merely said that his liver had failed and that it was caused by a disease he had. She started to cry, and as she was looking at the doctor in the casket she blurted out, "I'll find the nurse that did this to you if it's the last thing I do." We hugged again and then walked away. I looked at the casket and all of the photographs that BJ had brought to the funeral home and said to my partner, "Boy he looks bad."

Then I thought to myself about her comment. His liver had failed and she was going to find the nurse that did this to him. That didn't settle well. I began to think about what a nurse could do that would make him contract a disease that eventually made his liver fail.

My partner and I sat down behind—who else—Stella! She was in rare form with her usual jet-black dyed hair, and she was just chattering and gossiping with the gaggle of women around her.

As we sat there, I looked at the casket and thought about the doctor. He really looked bad. The color of his skin was horrible, and his face was sunken in. In just four months, he had gone downhill fast.

I noticed BJ with the video camera again. This time she was taking a video of all of the guests that came to pay their respects. She really was going off of the deep end, acting crazy as usual.

Sitting behind Stella, I waited for her to finish her conversation. I knew she would turn around and start talking at some point. Stella was sitting next to the funeral director's wife, Julia. They turned around to say hi, and we chatted for a few minutes when I made the comment, "he really looks bad; I didn't even know he was ill."

Julia turned and looked at me, saying, "honey, you don't even know how he died do you?" I replied by saying, "no, how did he die?" That's was all I had to say to open the floodgate. Julia proceeded to tell me that the doctor had put a gun under his chin and blown his face off. I said, "you've got to be kidding!" She said, "no, I'm not." I said, "why would he do that?" Julia said that apparently he had contracted the liver disease from a nurse that had given him a shot with a dirty needle. It was a flu shot, and at the time, there wasn't much concern and awareness in the community about using dirty needles. Making the matter worse was the doctor's drinking problem. When the liver disease was discovered, it was too late. There was nothing he could do, and in an effort to seek help, he was admitted to a well-known hospital to determine the extent of the damage. He spent three days there, and the prognosis was that 90 percent of his liver was gone. He had little time, and he was told that his quality of life would progressively diminish. The hospital suggested that he get on a liver transplant waiting list as soon as possible, telling him that he more than likely had trained the surgeons that would be performing the operation. The doctor flatly refused that option, knowing what those patients went through in the recovery stage. He maintained his selfishness to the bitter end. BJ had asked Stella to accompany her to the hospital when she admitted the doctor for testing, and the entire two-hour trip home was spent trying to convince him to have the transplant. He repeatedly refused to consider it.

They arrived home from the hospital on the Thursday afternoon before the doctor killed himself. BJ spent that time and all of her energy trying to make him comfortable and to convince him to have the transplant. He maintained that he knew what those patients went through, and he didn't want to go through that. By Sunday morning, BJ was beside herself as she told her husband that she was going to church. He replied that it was good for her to go to church, and he asked her to go get him a newspaper and some cough drops before that. BJ complied with his request and headed out of the door for the drugstore. When BJ returned from getting the paper and cough drops, she entered the foyer and noticed that the dogs weren't barking and coming to the door. She didn't see the doctor; she thought that he must be walking them in the backyard and didn't think much more about it. As she entered the bedroom to get dressed for church, she saw the two dogs on their bed. The dogs were shaking and acting very nervous. At that moment, she knew that something was wrong. She called out for her husband and there was no answer. She raced around the house, looking for him; he was nowhere to be found. Then she noticed that the basement door was open and that there was a light on. Again she called out for her husband, and again there was no answer. BJ raced down the stairs and suddenly noticed him lying on the floor in the corner. As she approached his lifeless body, she realized what he had done. She was horrified as she realized that his face was gone. Flesh and blood had been splattered all over the walls, and the gun was still in his hand. BJ frantically ran back up the stairway and grabbed the phone and dialed 911. The police and emergency squad arrived minutes later, only to find the doctor dead at the scene. BJ was a complete physical and mental wreck.

Weeks later, I drove past the house, thinking of the fun times that we had had. All of those thoughts were overshadowed by the thought of what he did in the basement. I noted that several weeks later, a pool was being added to the backyard. This was a wish of BJ's that the doctor hadn't wanted any part of, and he had made this quite clear.

It's been several years since the doctor's death, and I think of BJ often. She ended up with all of the money she needed and has moved to another city. She no longer had to put up with her husband's verbal and physical abuse. She was able to sell the cars and the house to live a dream life. I reflected upon the situation, thinking that she couldn't have wished for a better ending. I know there were times when she was just ready to kill him herself for the way he treated her. Maybe she did wish for it. Maybe her wish did come true. No one will ever know except her. As for me, I kept the job answering customer calls at the insurance company, and I often think of how it could have been. I had a blast while it lasted, even though the doctor was a jerk at times.

As you go through life, you realize that things do happen for a reason. I had wished for an opportunity, and I was able to experience it both as a professional chauffeur and as a private chauffeur. There was a lot I didn't like, and maybe that was the true lesson I was to learn for myself. I guess I did have that golden opportunity after all.

Remember to fasten your seat belt!

Printed in the United States
204974BV00001B/8/A

9 781434 340467